STAR WARS

THE CLONE WARS

THE ENEMY WITHIN

DESIGNER KRYSTAL HENNES

ASSISTANT EDITOR FREDDYE LINS

EDITOR RANDY STRADLEY

PUBLISHER MIKE RICHARDSON

Special thanks to Joanne Chan Taylor, Leland Chee, Troy Alders, Carol Roeder, Jann Moorhead, and David Anderman at Lucas Licensing.

Published by Dark Horse Books, a division of Dark Horse Comics, Inc.
10956 SE Main Street, Milwaukie, OR 97222

DarkHorse.com | StarWars.com

To find a comics shop in your area, call the Comic Shop Locator Service toll-free at 1.888.266.4226
First edition: March 2012 | ISBN 978-1-59582-845-3

10 9 8 7 6 5 4 3 2 1

PRINTED AT 1010 PRINTING INTERNATIONAL, LTD., GUANGDONG PROVINCE, CHINA

Library of Congress Cataloging-in-Publication Data

Barlow, Jeremy.
Star wars, the clone wars : the enemy within / script, Jeremy Barlow ; art, Brian Koschak ; colors, Mae Hao ; lettering, Michael Heisler ; cover art, Brian Koschak. -- 1st ed.
  p. cm. -- (Star wars : the clone wars)
Summary: "Tasked with ending the fighting on a war-torn world, a platoon of Clone Troopers find their plans undone, but must still continue their flawed mission"--Provided by publisher.
ISBN 978-1-59582-845-3
1. Graphic novels. I. Koschak, Brian, ill. II. Title. III. Title: Enemy within.
PZ7.7.B36Ssm 2012
741.5'973--dc22
                    2011038196

STAR WARS: THE CLONE WARS—THE ENEMY WITHIN

STAR WARS

THE CLONE WARS

THE ENEMY WITHIN

SCRIPT **JEREMY BARLOW**

ART **BRIAN KOSCHAK**

COLORS **MAE HAO**
MARLON ILAGAN

LETTERING **MICHAEL HEISLER**

COVER ART **BRIAN KOSCHAK**

DARK HORSE BOOKS®

THE RISE OF THE EMPIRE
1000–0 YEARS BEFORE *STAR WARS: A NEW HOPE*

The events in these stories take place approximately twenty-two years before the Battle of Yavin.

After the seeming final defeat of the Sith, the Republic enters a state of complacency. In the waning years of the Republic, the Senate is rife with corruption, and the ambitious Senator Palpatine has himself elected Supreme Chancellor. This is the era of the prequel trilogy.

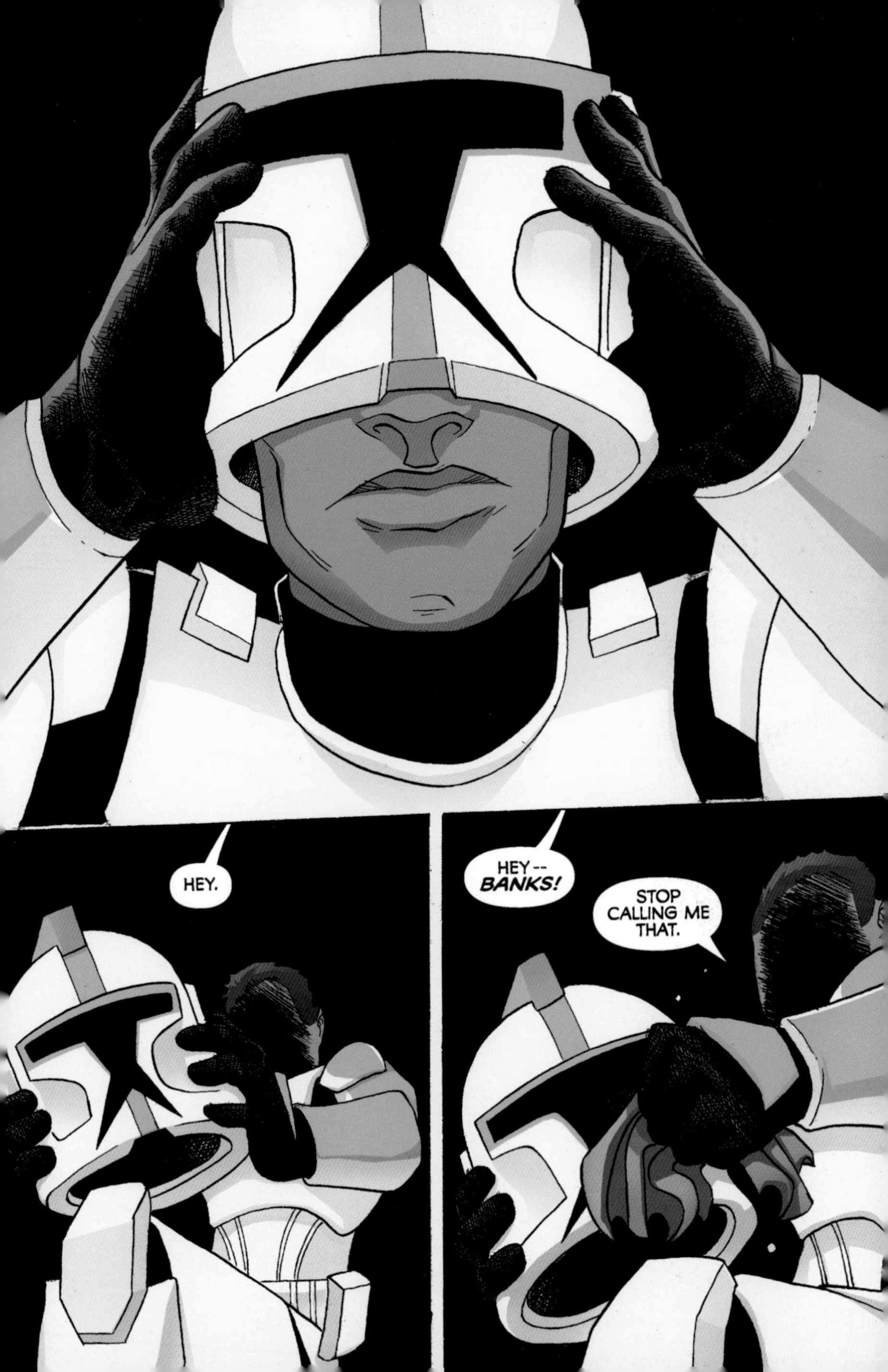
HEY.
HEY -- *BANKS!*
STOP CALLING ME THAT.

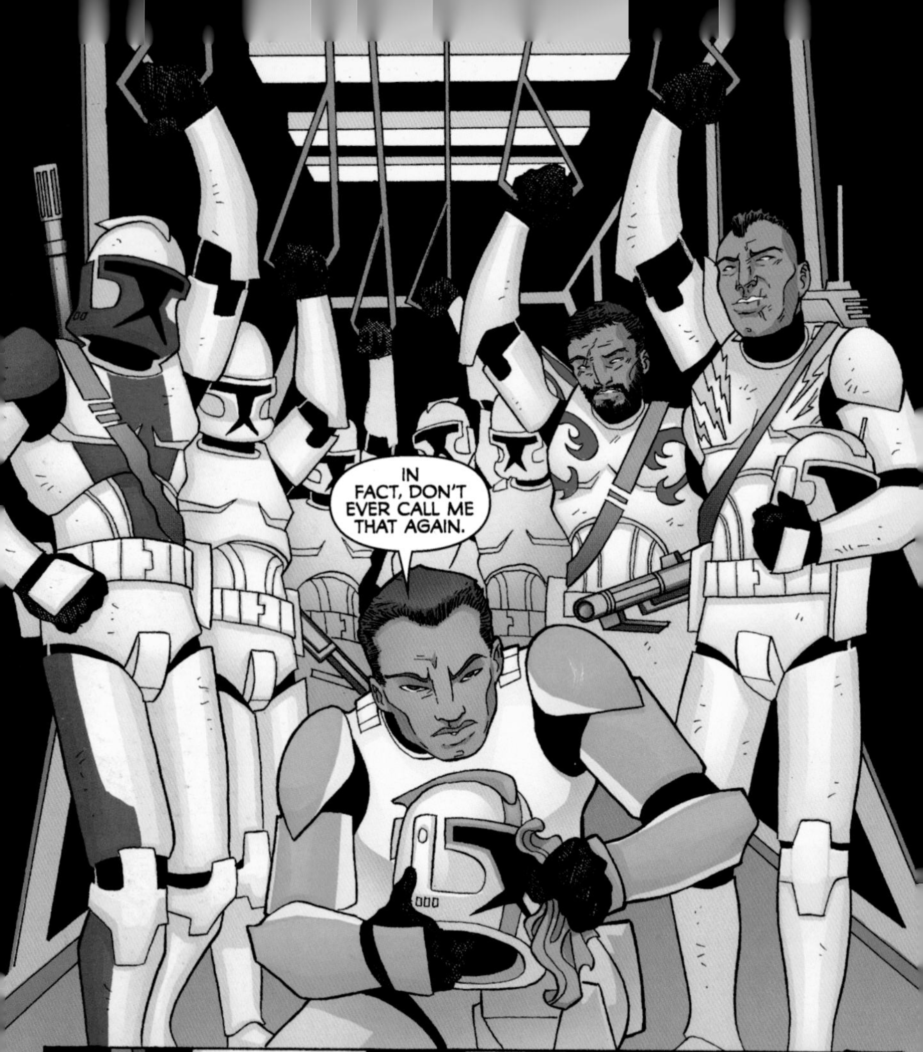
IN FACT, DON'T EVER CALL ME THAT AGAIN.

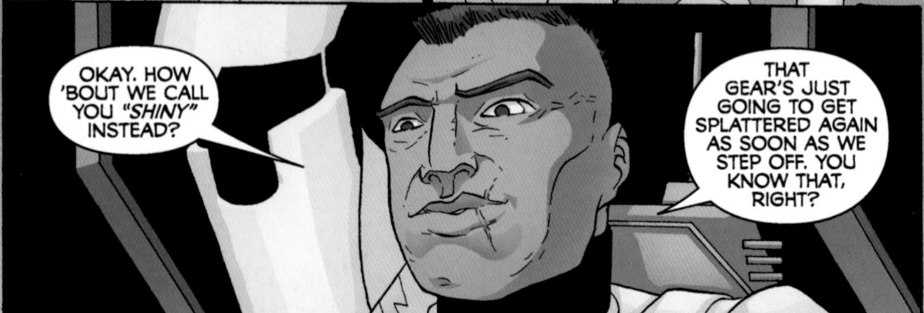
OKAY. HOW 'BOUT WE CALL YOU "SHINY" INSTEAD?
THAT GEAR'S JUST GOING TO GET SPLATTERED AGAIN AS SOON AS WE STEP OFF. YOU KNOW THAT, RIGHT?

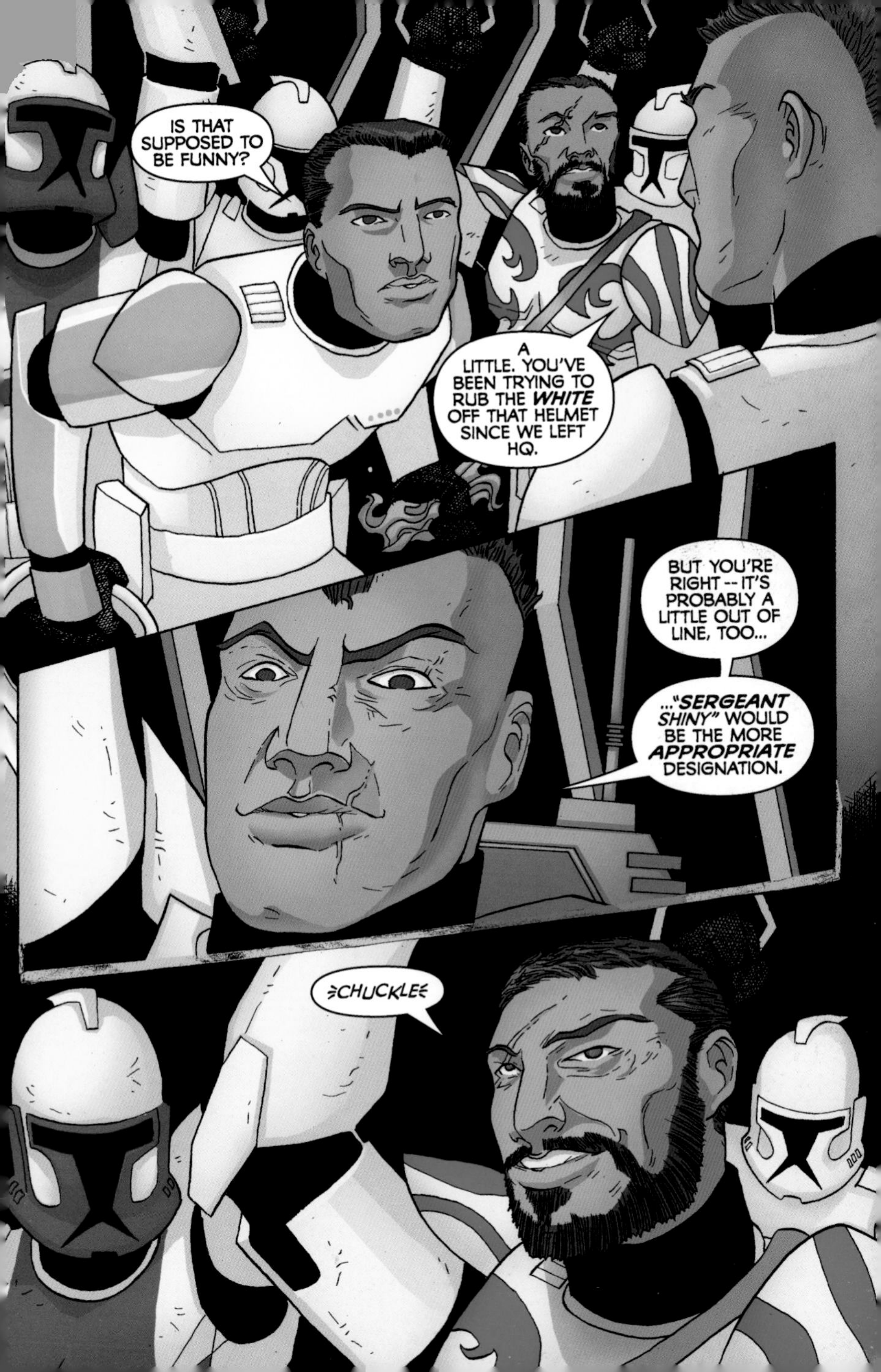
IS THAT SUPPOSED TO BE FUNNY?
A LITTLE. YOU'VE BEEN TRYING TO RUB THE *WHITE* OFF THAT HELMET SINCE WE LEFT HQ.
BUT YOU'RE RIGHT -- IT'S PROBABLY A LITTLE OUT OF LINE, TOO...
..."*SERGEANT SHINY*" WOULD BE THE MORE *APPROPRIATE* DESIGNATION.
CHUCKLE

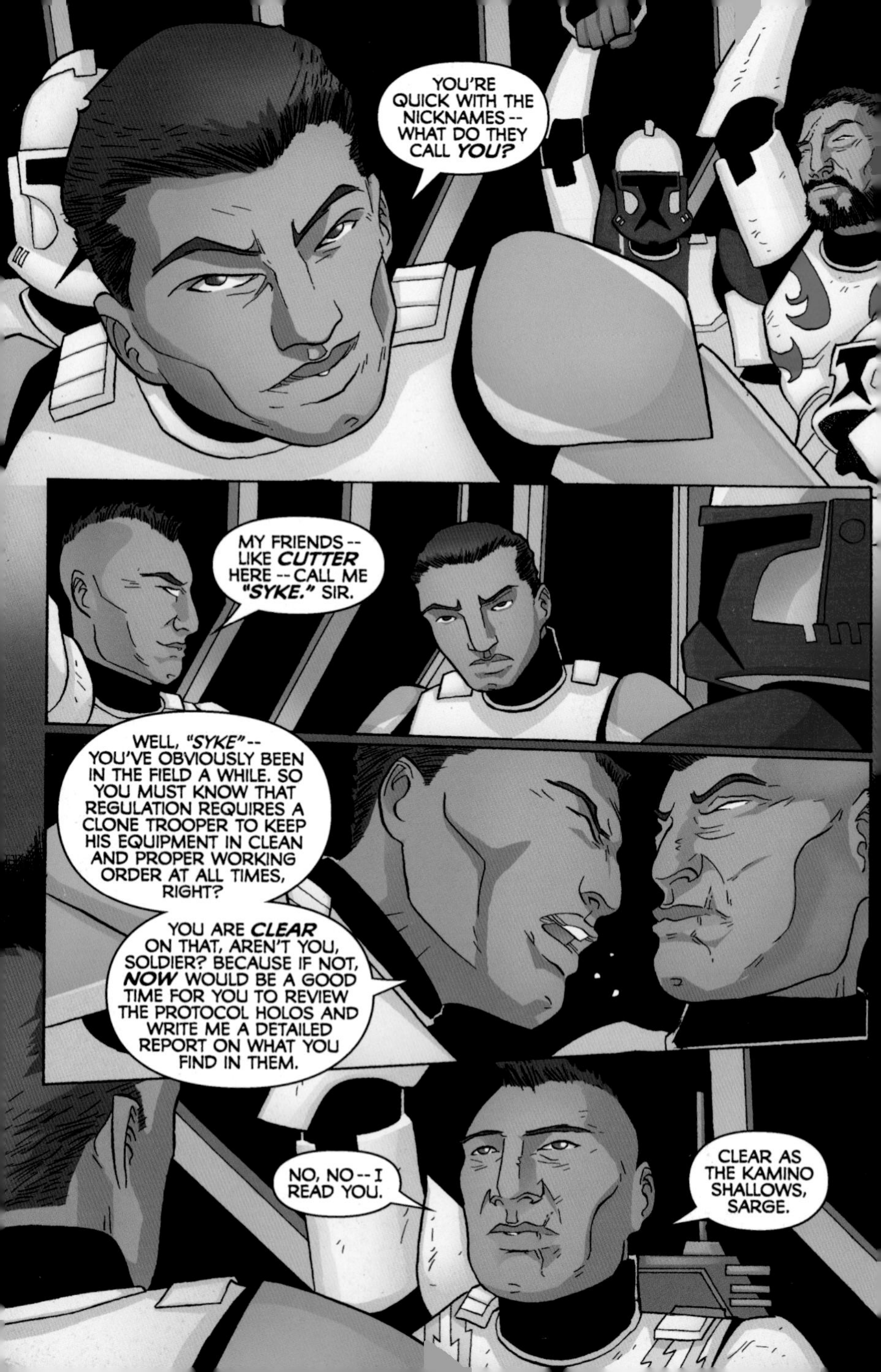
YOU'RE QUICK WITH THE NICKNAMES -- WHAT DO THEY CALL *YOU?*
MY FRIENDS -- LIKE *CUTTER* HERE -- CALL ME *"SYKE."* SIR.
WELL, *"SYKE"* -- YOU'VE OBVIOUSLY BEEN IN THE FIELD A WHILE. SO YOU MUST KNOW THAT REGULATION REQUIRES A CLONE TROOPER TO KEEP HIS EQUIPMENT IN CLEAN AND PROPER WORKING ORDER AT ALL TIMES, RIGHT?
YOU ARE *CLEAR* ON THAT, AREN'T YOU, SOLDIER? BECAUSE IF NOT, *NOW* WOULD BE A GOOD TIME FOR YOU TO REVIEW THE PROTOCOL HOLOS AND WRITE ME A DETAILED REPORT ON WHAT YOU FIND IN THEM.
NO, NO -- I READ YOU.
CLEAR AS THE KAMINO SHALLOWS, SARGE.

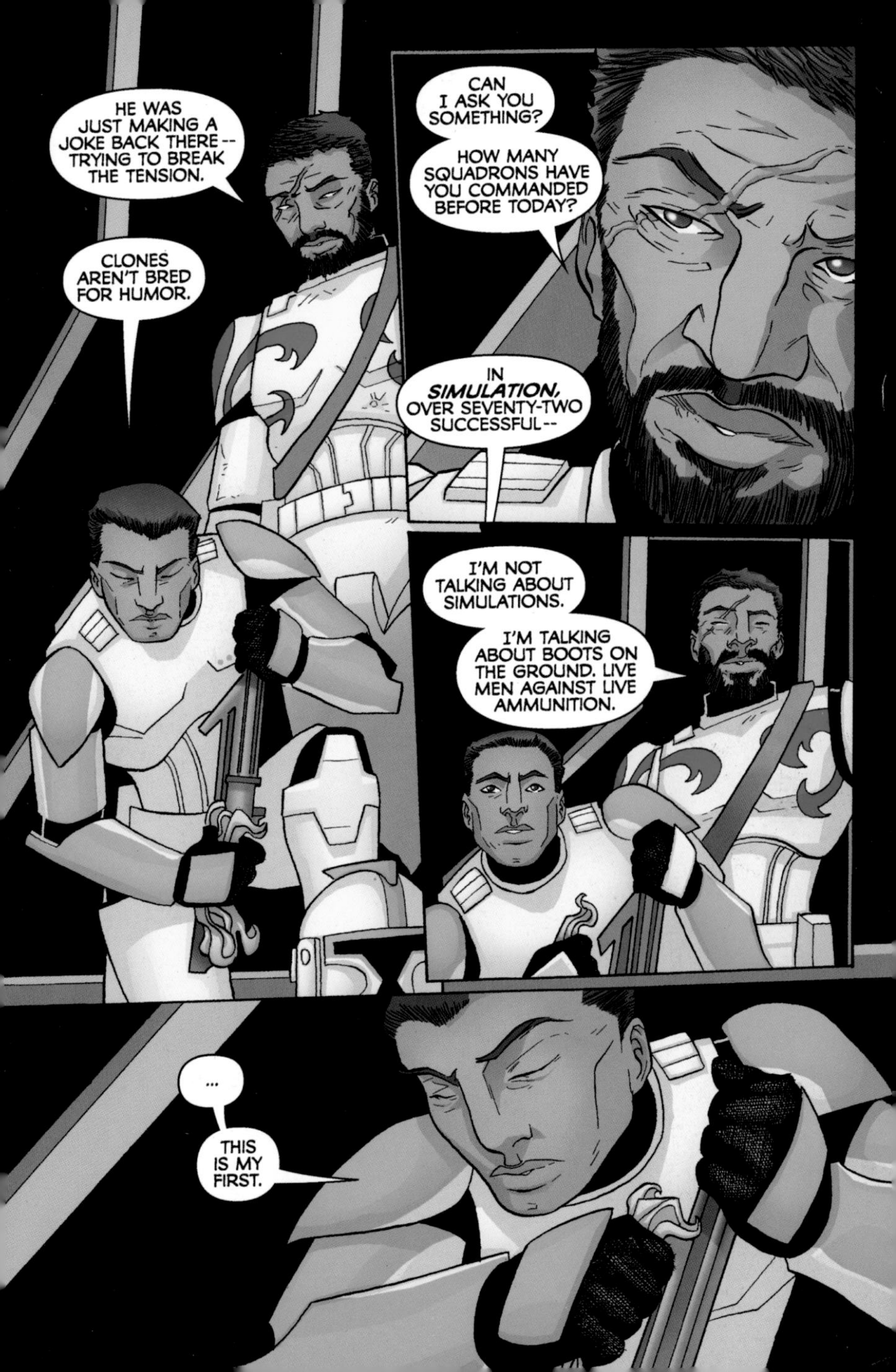

HE WAS JUST MAKING A JOKE BACK THERE -- TRYING TO BREAK THE TENSION.
CLONES AREN'T BRED FOR HUMOR.
CAN I ASK YOU SOMETHING?
HOW MANY SQUADRONS HAVE YOU COMMANDED BEFORE TODAY?
IN *SIMULATION,* OVER SEVENTY-TWO SUCCESSFUL--
I'M NOT TALKING ABOUT SIMULATIONS.
I'M TALKING ABOUT BOOTS ON THE GROUND. LIVE MEN AGAINST LIVE AMMUNITION.
...
THIS IS MY FIRST.

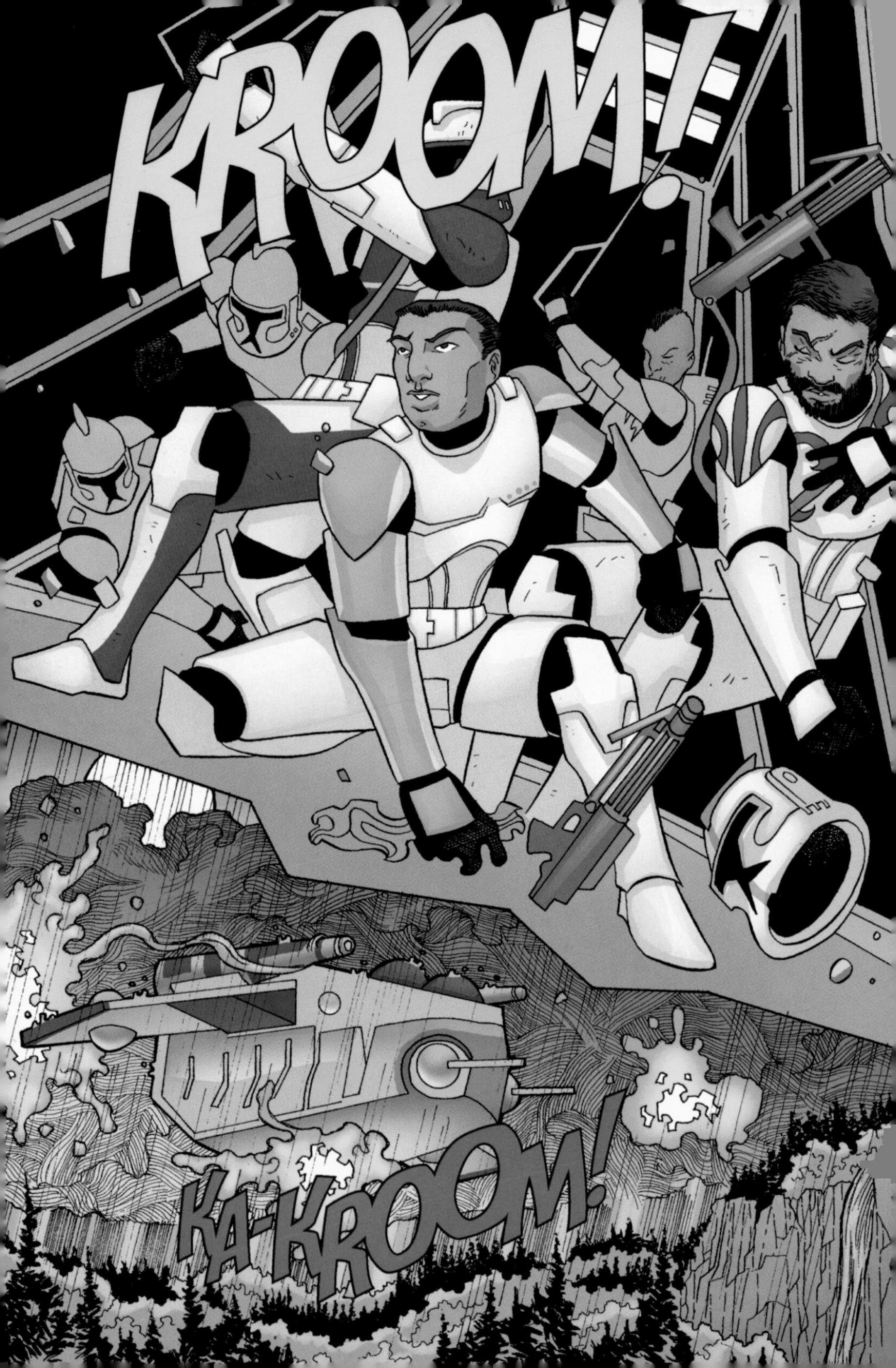
KROOM!
KA-KROOM!

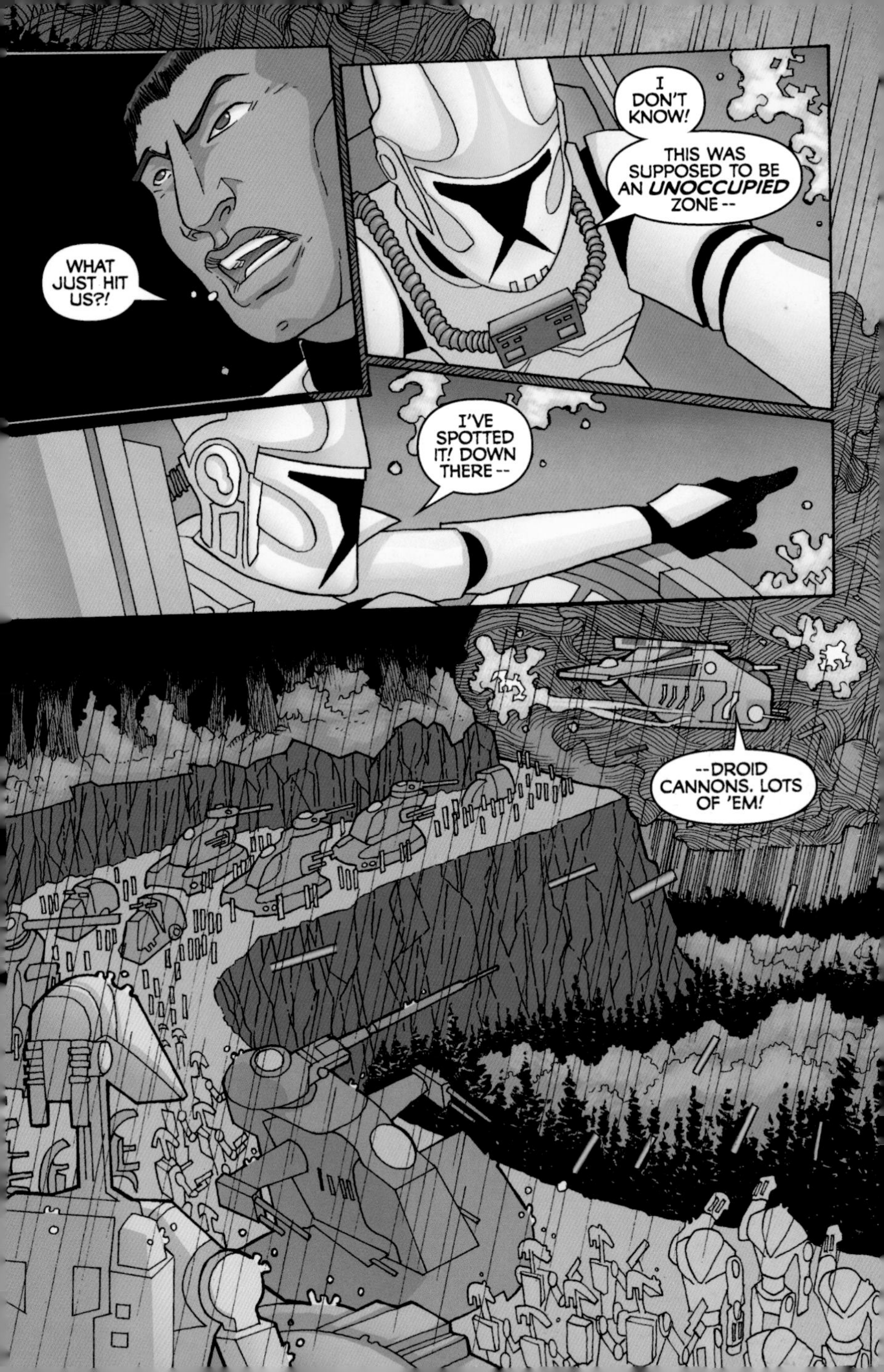
WHAT JUST HIT US?!
I DON'T KNOW!
THIS WAS SUPPOSED TO BE AN *UNOCCUPIED* ZONE --
I'VE SPOTTED IT! DOWN THERE --
--DROID CANNONS. LOTS OF 'EM!

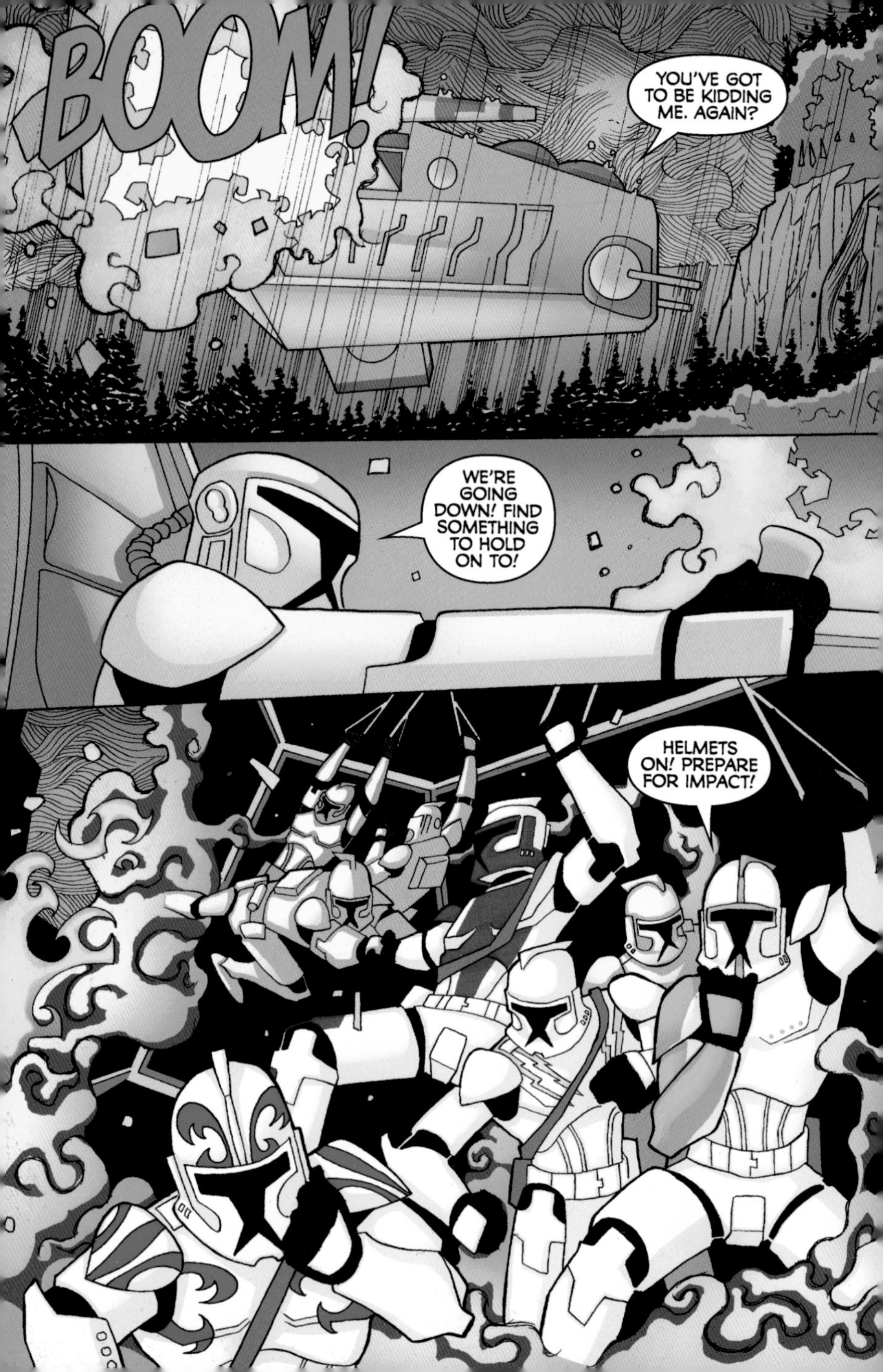
BOOM!
YOU'VE GOT TO BE KIDDING ME. AGAIN?
WE'RE GOING DOWN! FIND SOMETHING TO HOLD ON TO!
HELMETS ON! PREPARE FOR IMPACT!

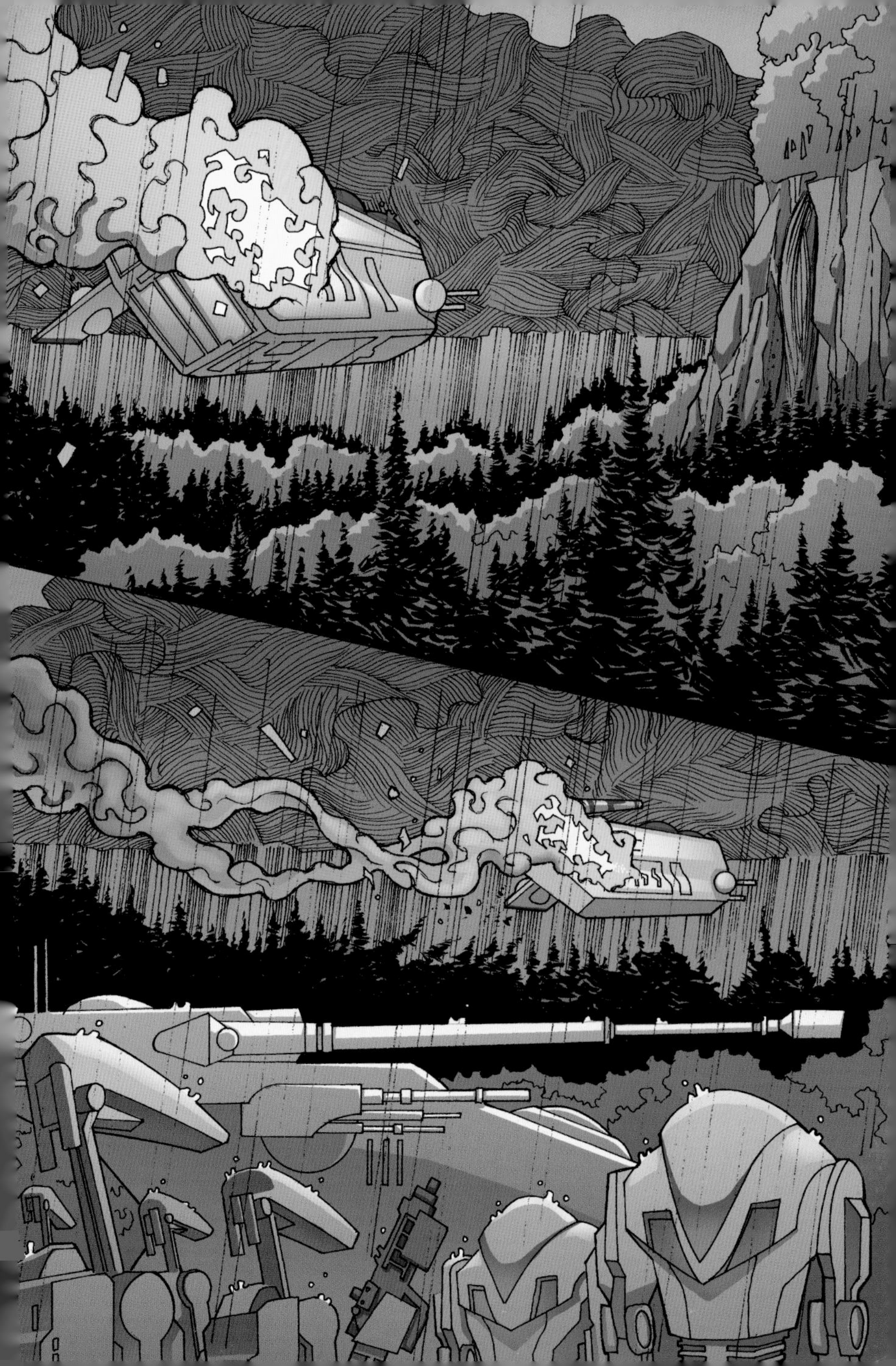

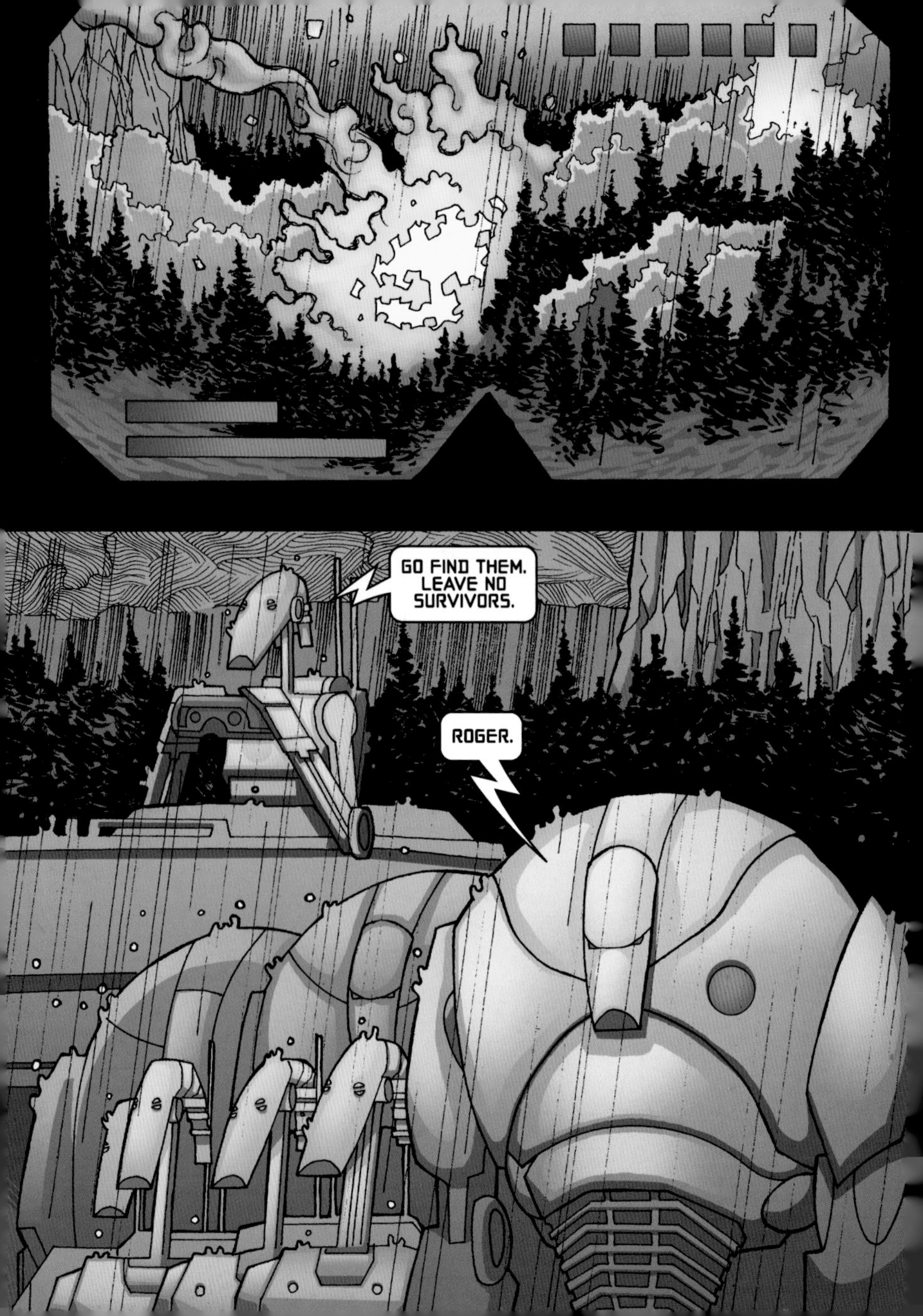
GO FIND THEM. LEAVE NO SURVIVORS.
ROGER.

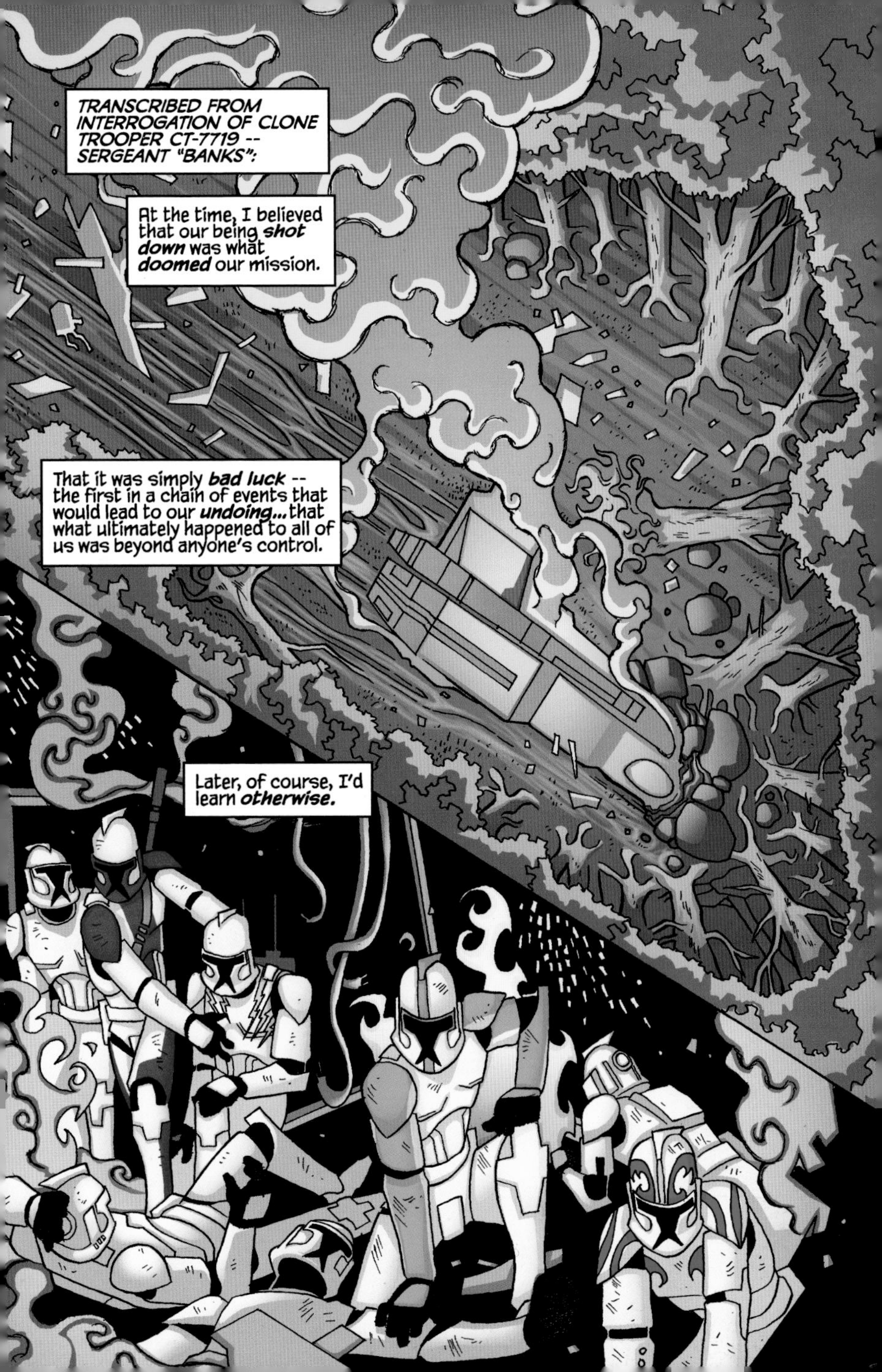
TRANSCRIBED FROM INTERROGATION OF CLONE TROOPER CT-7719 -- SERGEANT "BANKS":
At the time, I believed that our being *shot down* was what *doomed* our mission.
That it was simply *bad luck* -- the first in a chain of events that would lead to our *undoing*... that what ultimately happened to all of us was beyond anyone's control.
Later, of course, I'd learn *otherwise.*

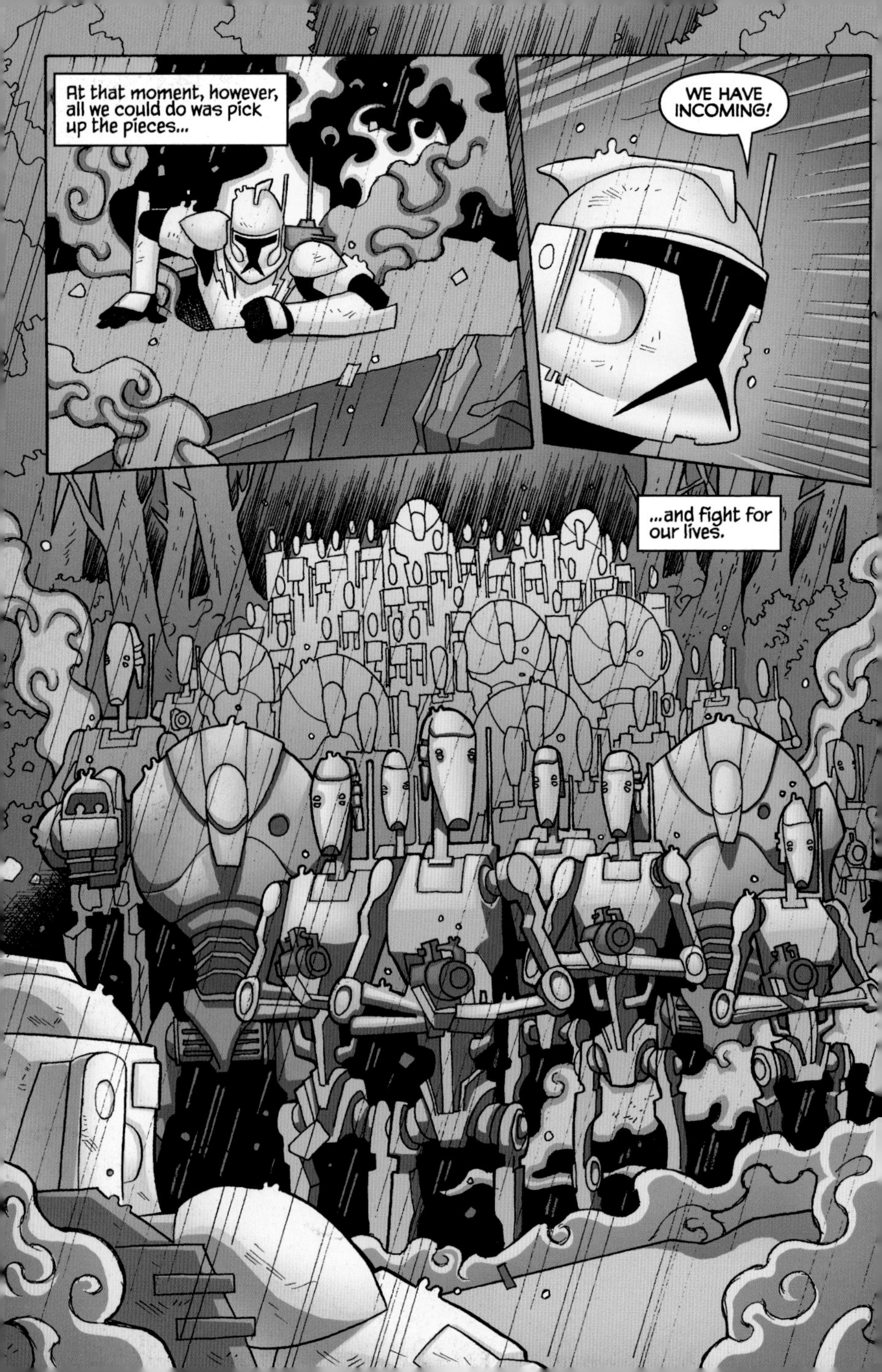
At that moment, however, all we could do was pick up the pieces...
WE HAVE INCOMING!
...and fight for our lives.

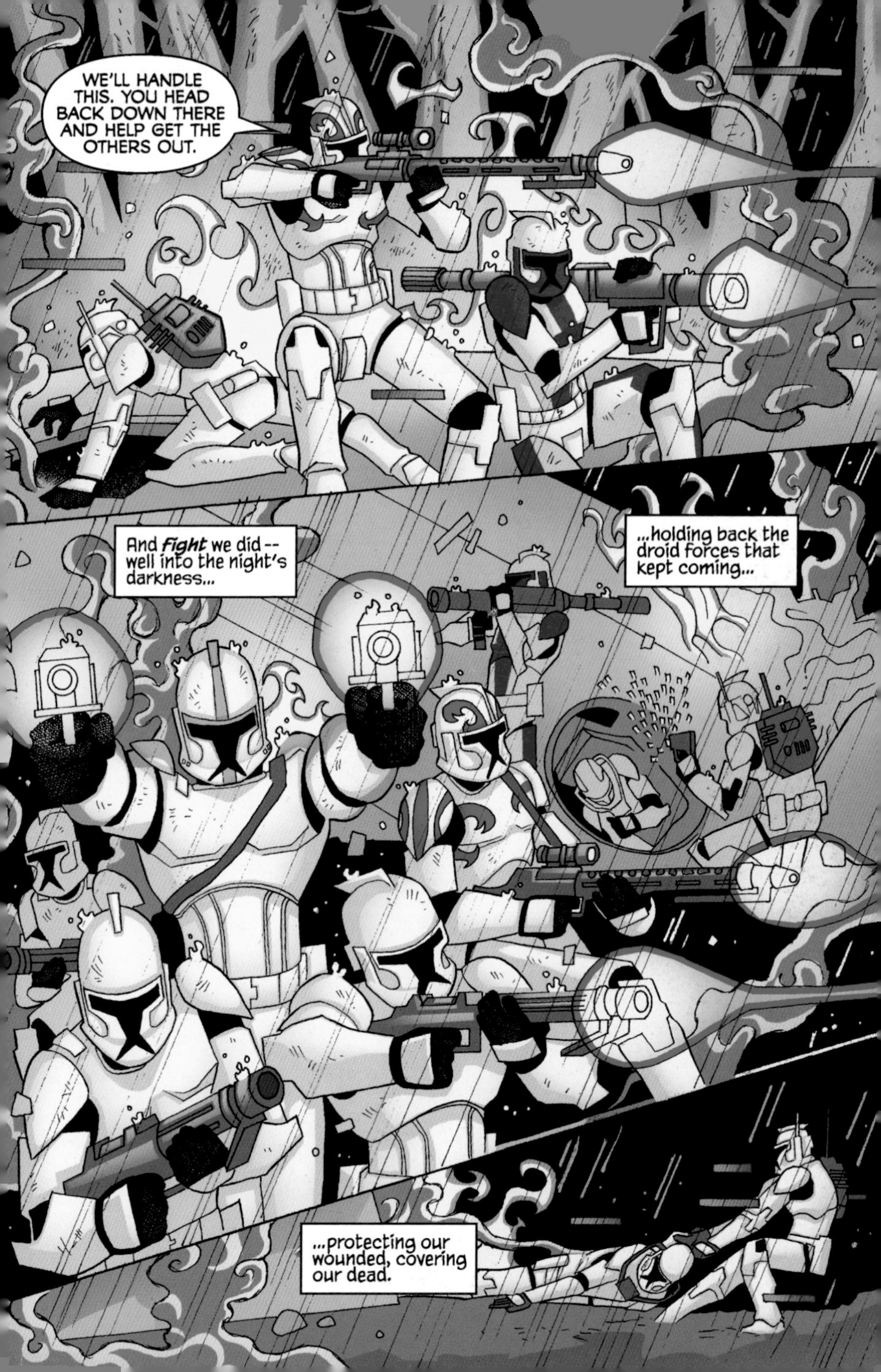
WE'LL HANDLE THIS. YOU HEAD BACK DOWN THERE AND HELP GET THE OTHERS OUT.
And *Fight* we did -- well into the night's darkness...
...holding back the droid forces that kept coming...
...protecting our wounded, covering our dead.

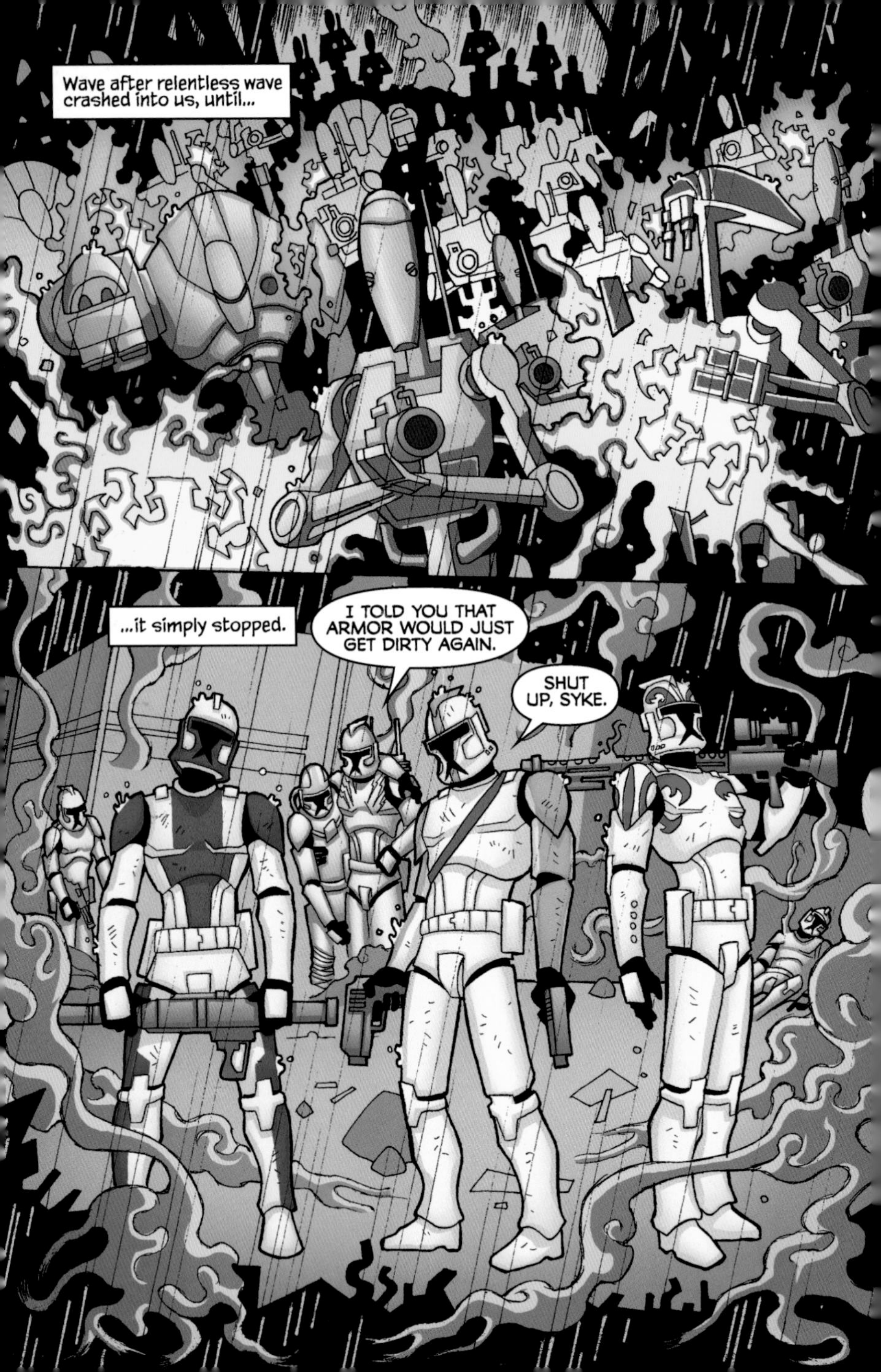
Wave after relentless wave crashed into us, until...
...it simply stopped.
I TOLD YOU THAT ARMOR WOULD JUST GET DIRTY AGAIN.
SHUT UP, SYKE.

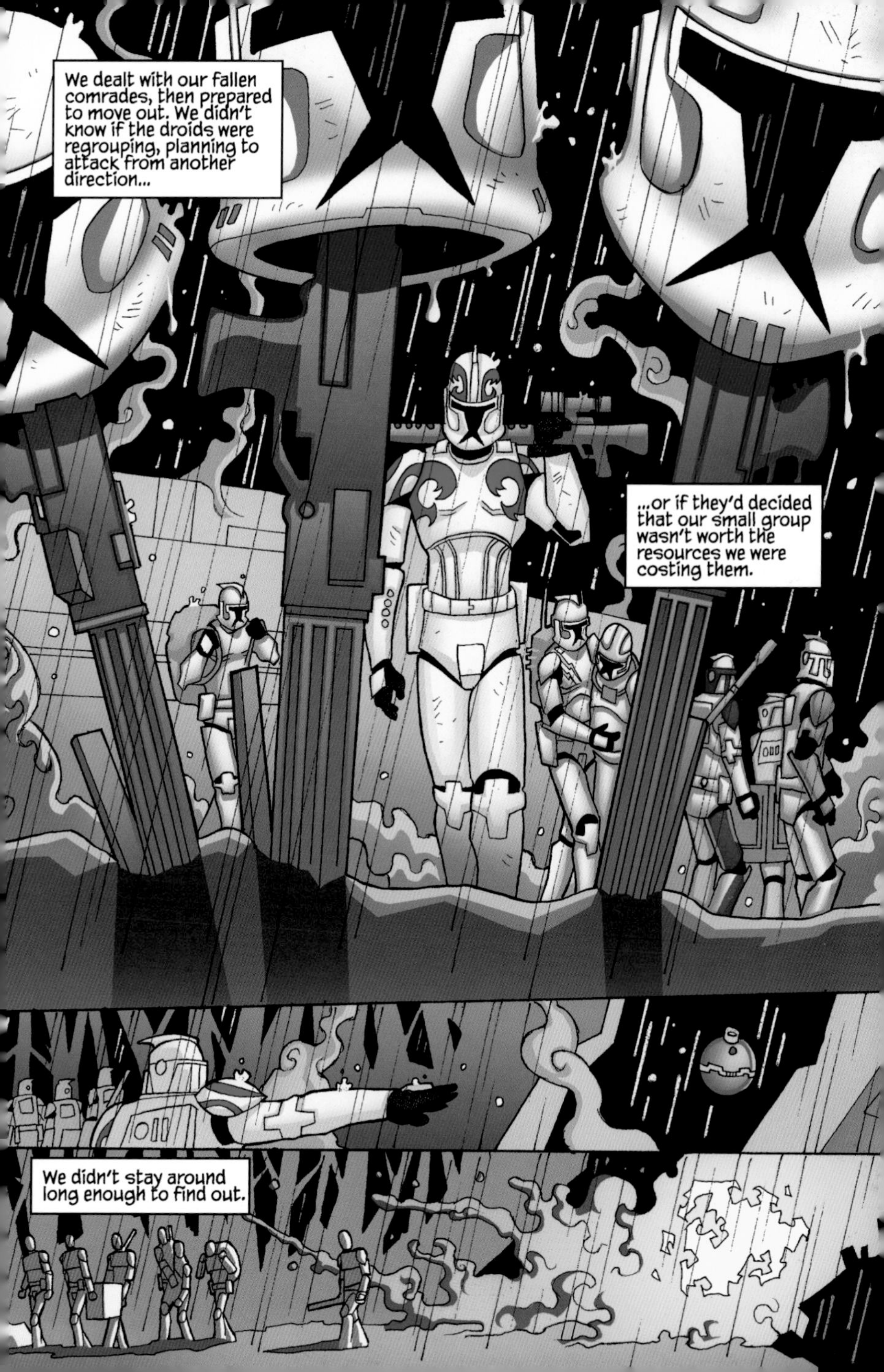
We dealt with our fallen comrades, then prepared to move out. We didn't know if the droids were regrouping, planning to attack from another direction...
...or if they'd decided that our small group wasn't worth the resources we were costing them.
We didn't stay around long enough to find out.

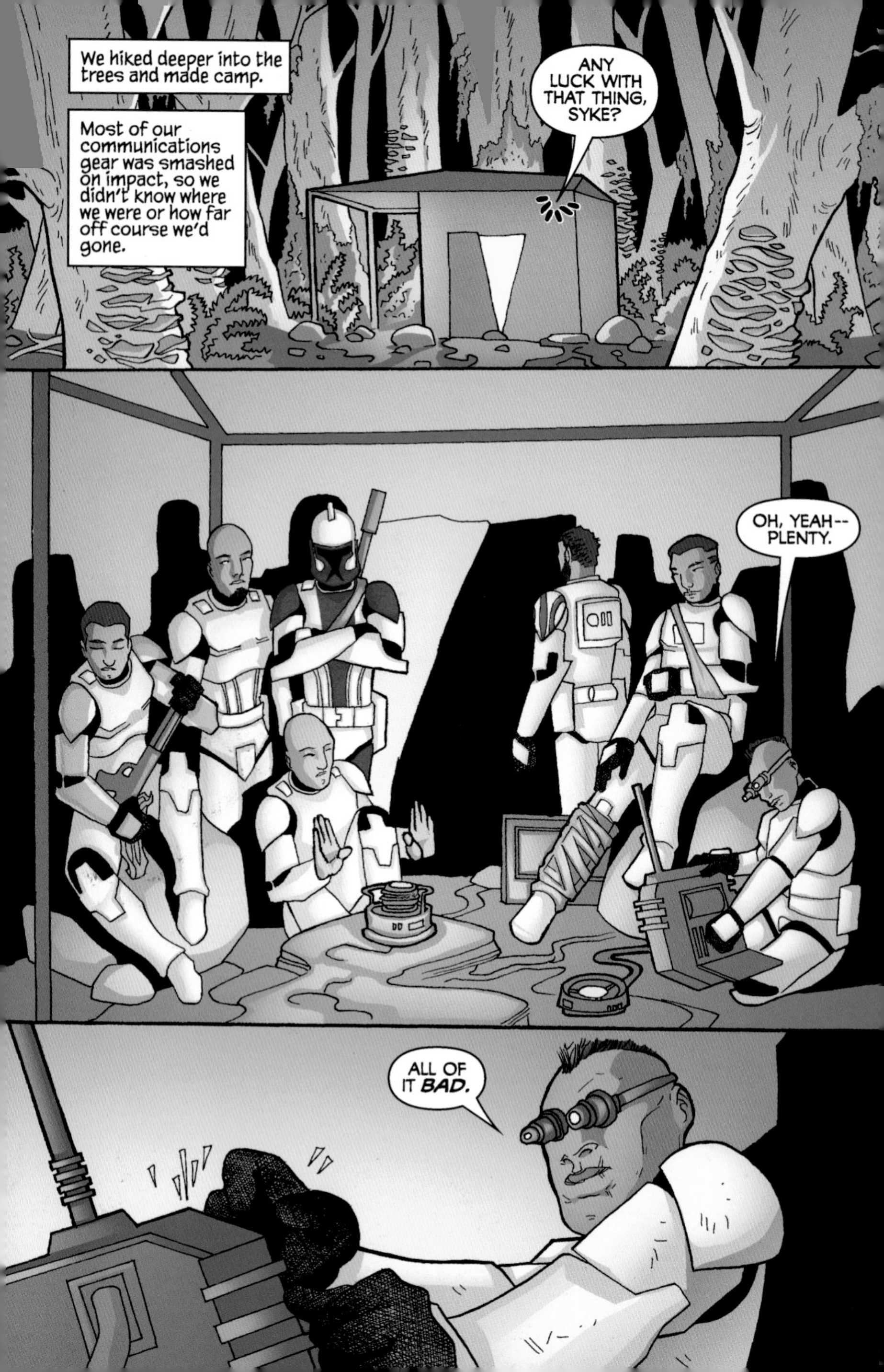
We hiked deeper into the trees and made camp.
Most of our communications gear was smashed on impact, so we didn't know where we were or how far off course we'd gone.
ANY LUCK WITH THAT THING, SYKE?
OH, YEAH-- PLENTY.
ALL OF IT *BAD.*

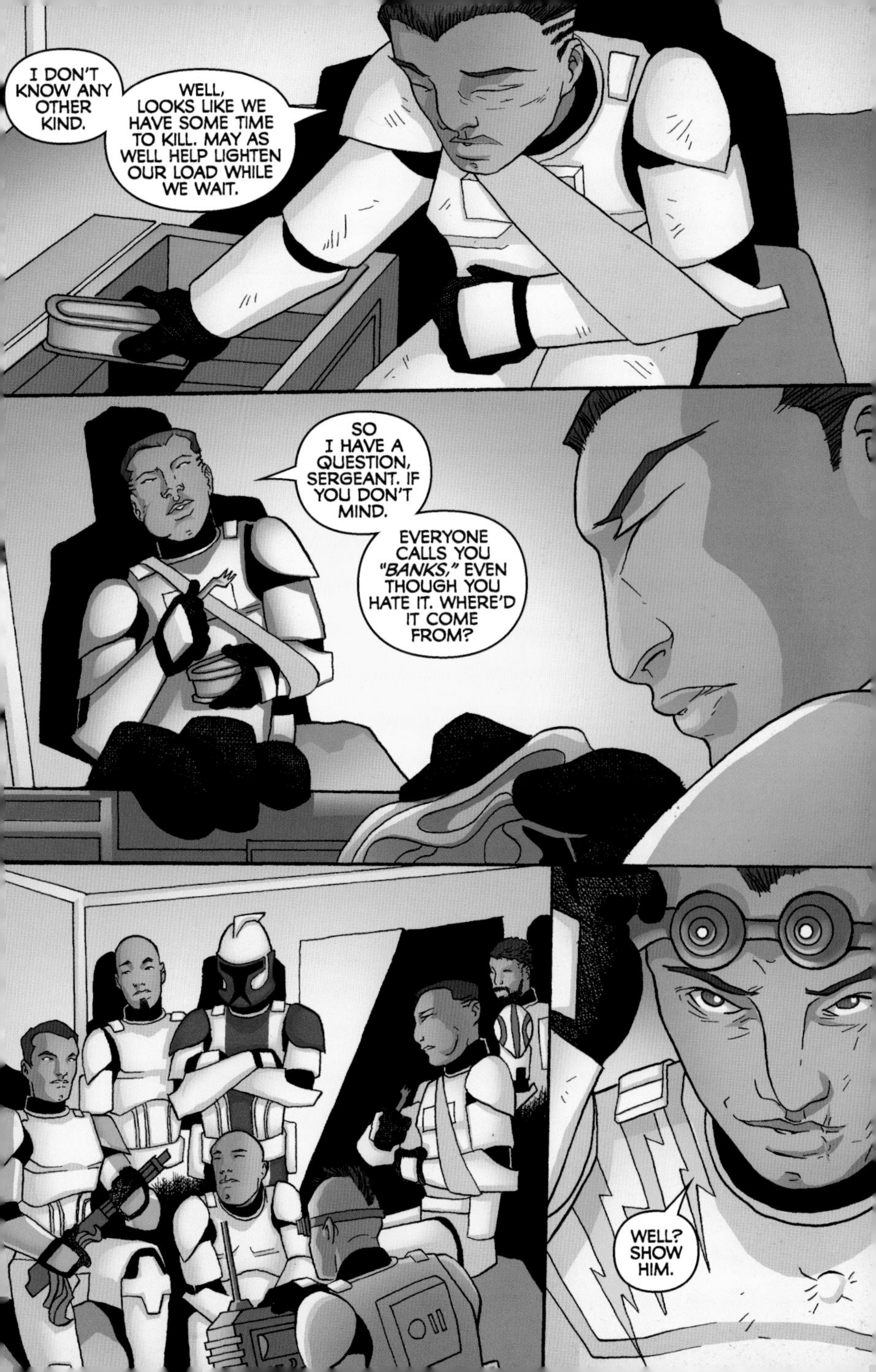
I DON'T KNOW ANY OTHER KIND.
WELL, LOOKS LIKE WE HAVE SOME TIME TO KILL. MAY AS WELL HELP LIGHTEN OUR LOAD WHILE WE WAIT.
SO I HAVE A QUESTION, SERGEANT. IF YOU DON'T MIND.
EVERYONE CALLS YOU *"BANKS,"* EVEN THOUGH YOU HATE IT. WHERE'D IT COME FROM?
WELL? SHOW HIM.

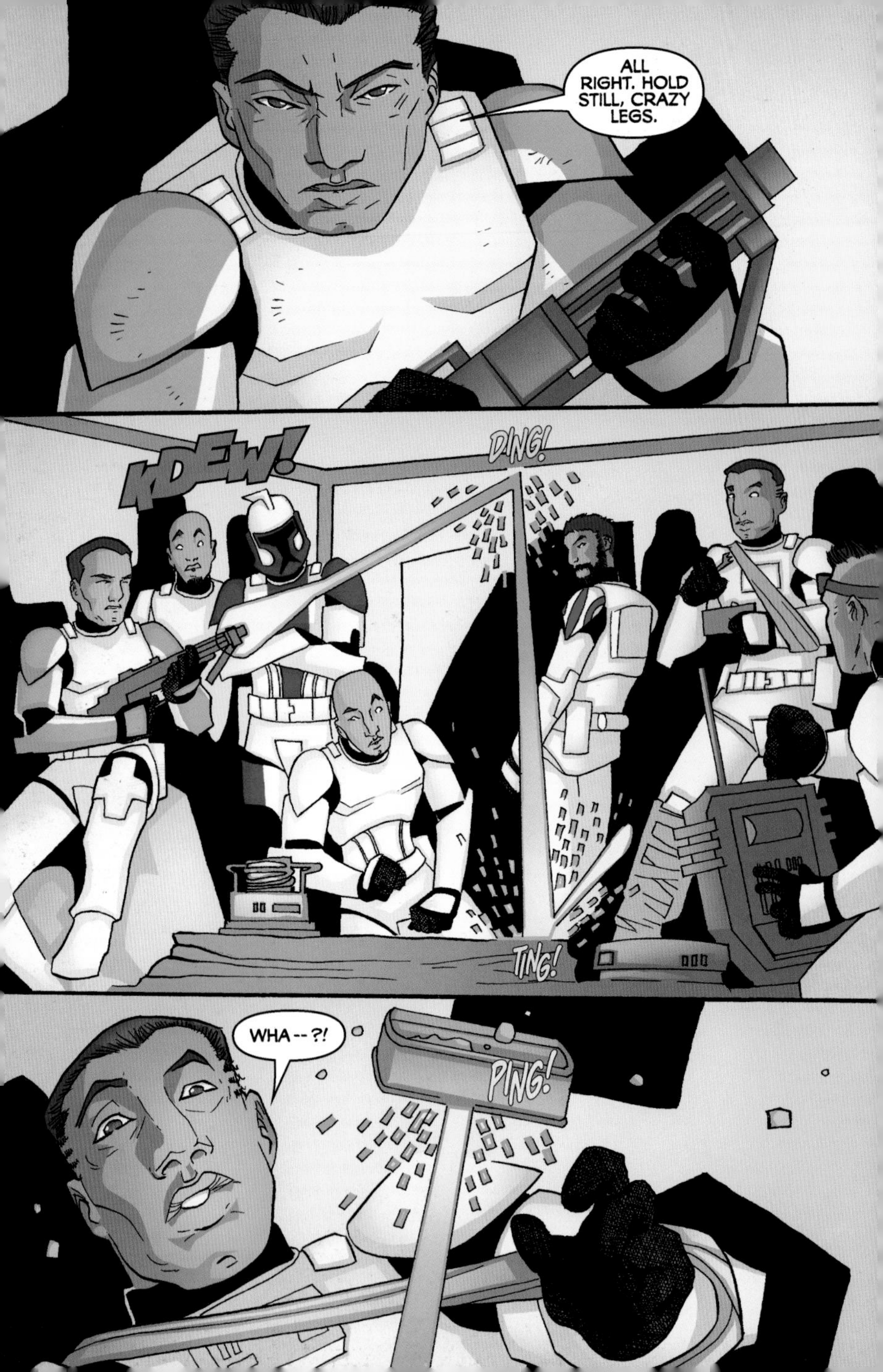
ALL RIGHT. HOLD STILL, CRAZY LEGS.
KDEW!
DING!
TING!
WHA -- ?!
PING!

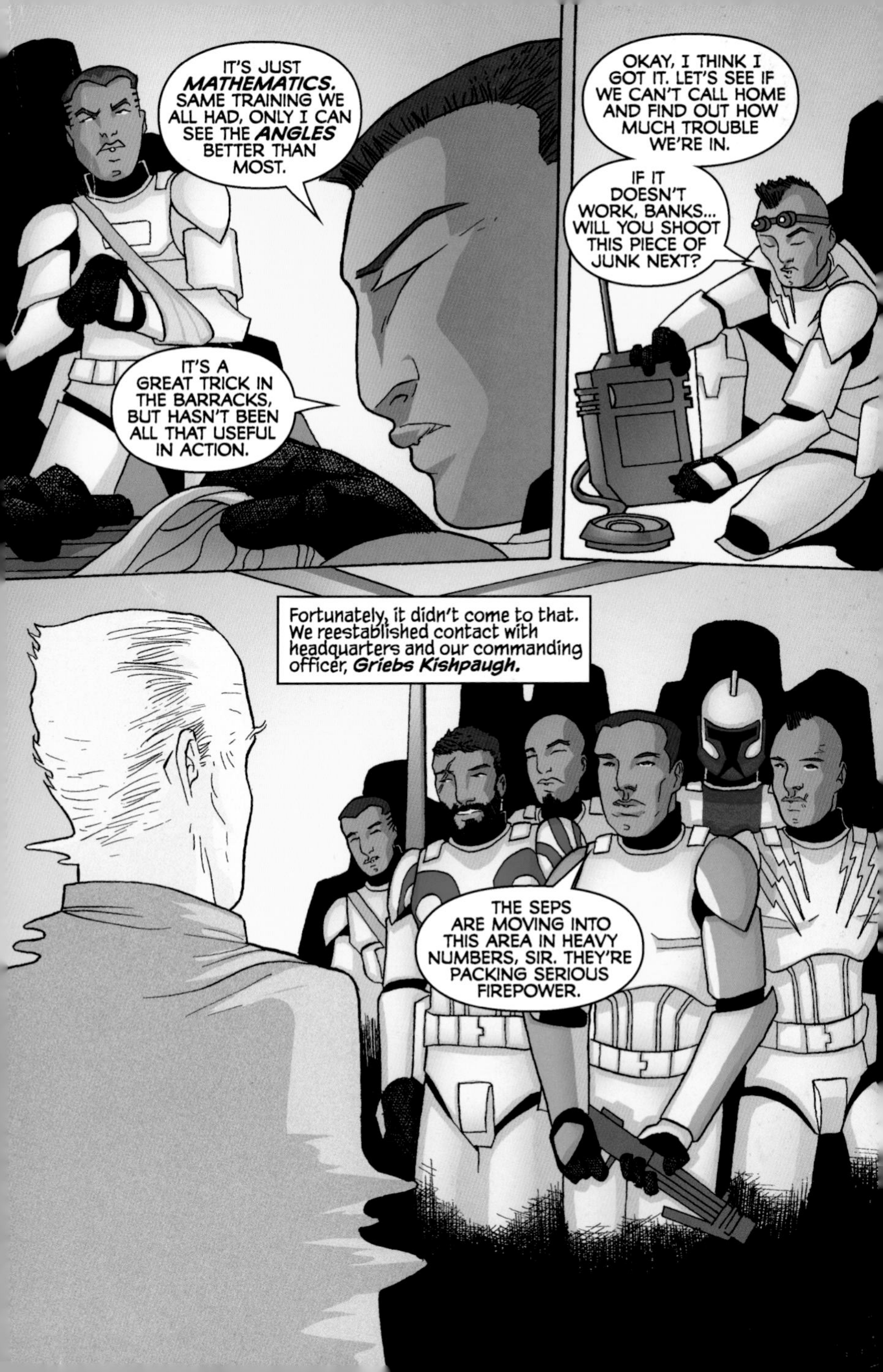
IT'S JUST MATHEMATICS. SAME TRAINING WE ALL HAD, ONLY I CAN SEE THE ANGLES BETTER THAN MOST.
IT'S A GREAT TRICK IN THE BARRACKS, BUT HASN'T BEEN ALL THAT USEFUL IN ACTION.
OKAY, I THINK I GOT IT. LET'S SEE IF WE CAN'T CALL HOME AND FIND OUT HOW MUCH TROUBLE WE'RE IN.
IF IT DOESN'T WORK, BANKS... WILL YOU SHOOT THIS PIECE OF JUNK NEXT?
Fortunately, it didn't come to that. We reestablished contact with headquarters and our commanding officer, Griebs Kishpaugh.
THE SEPS ARE MOVING INTO THIS AREA IN HEAVY NUMBERS, SIR. THEY'RE PACKING SERIOUS FIREPOWER.

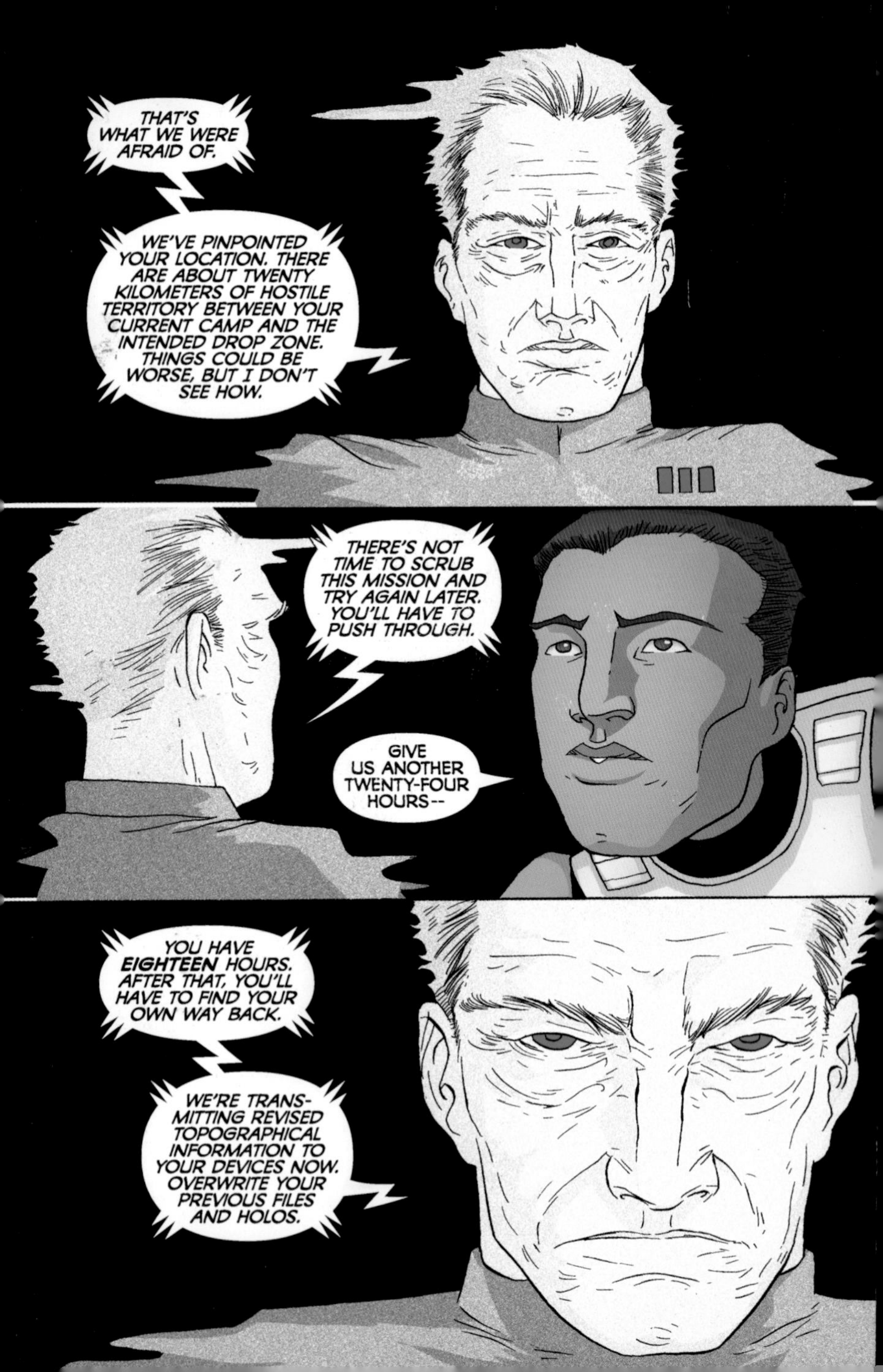
THAT'S WHAT WE WERE AFRAID OF.
WE'VE PINPOINTED YOUR LOCATION. THERE ARE ABOUT TWENTY KILOMETERS OF HOSTILE TERRITORY BETWEEN YOUR CURRENT CAMP AND THE INTENDED DROP ZONE. THINGS COULD BE WORSE, BUT I DON'T SEE HOW.
THERE'S NOT TIME TO SCRUB THIS MISSION AND TRY AGAIN LATER. YOU'LL HAVE TO PUSH THROUGH.
GIVE US ANOTHER TWENTY-FOUR HOURS--
YOU HAVE **EIGHTEEN** HOURS. AFTER THAT, YOU'LL HAVE TO FIND YOUR OWN WAY BACK.
WE'RE TRANS-MITTING REVISED TOPOGRAPHICAL INFORMATION TO YOUR DEVICES NOW. OVERWRITE YOUR PREVIOUS FILES AND HOLOS.

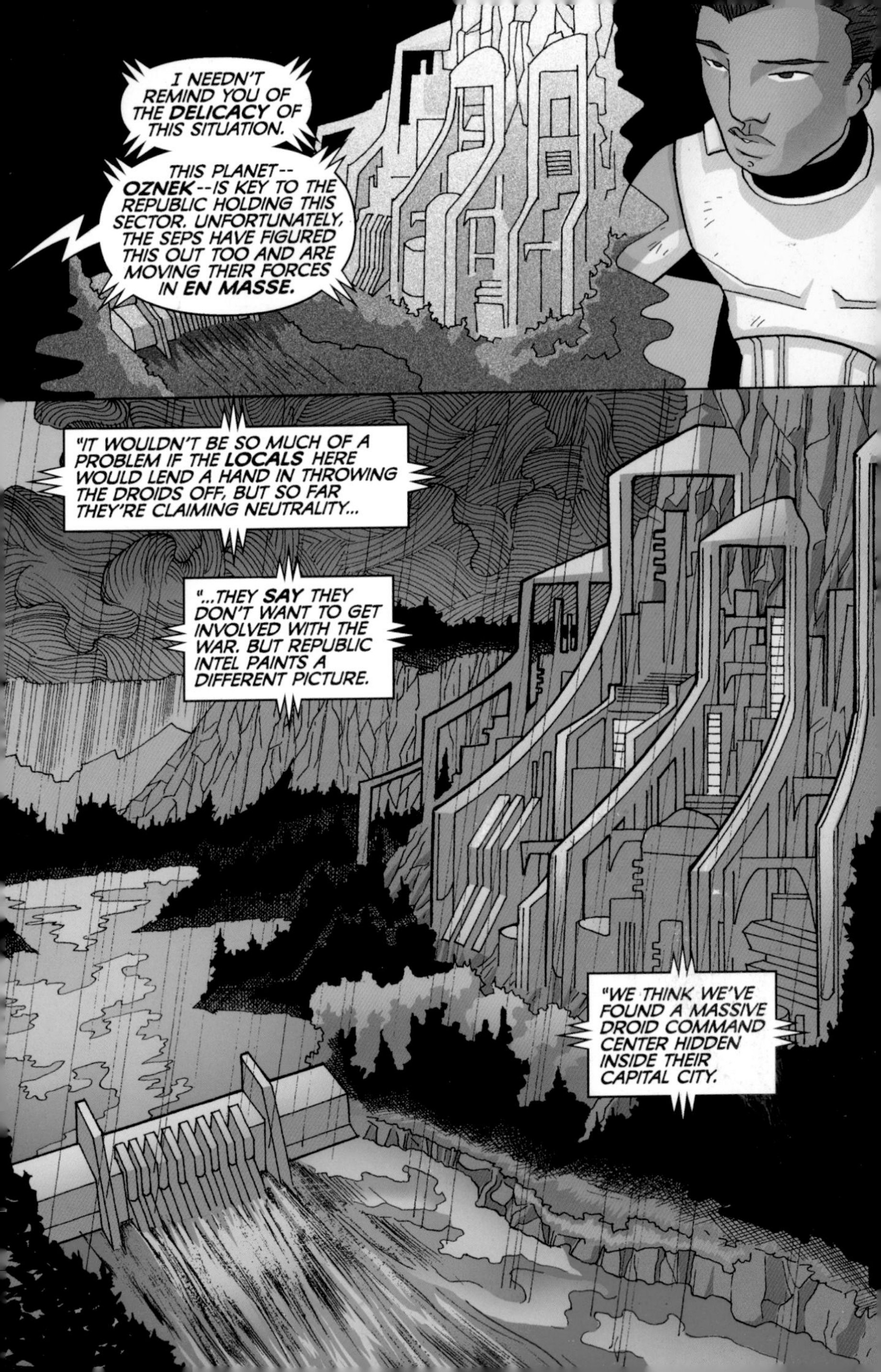
I NEEDN'T REMIND YOU OF THE DELICACY OF THIS SITUATION.
THIS PLANET-- OZNEK--IS KEY TO THE REPUBLIC HOLDING THIS SECTOR. UNFORTUNATELY, THE SEPS HAVE FIGURED THIS OUT TOO AND ARE MOVING THEIR FORCES IN EN MASSE.
"IT WOULDN'T BE SO MUCH OF A PROBLEM IF THE LOCALS HERE WOULD LEND A HAND IN THROWING THE DROIDS OFF, BUT SO FAR THEY'RE CLAIMING NEUTRALITY...
"...THEY SAY THEY DON'T WANT TO GET INVOLVED WITH THE WAR. BUT REPUBLIC INTEL PAINTS A DIFFERENT PICTURE.
"WE THINK WE'VE FOUND A MASSIVE DROID COMMAND CENTER HIDDEN INSIDE THEIR CAPITAL CITY.

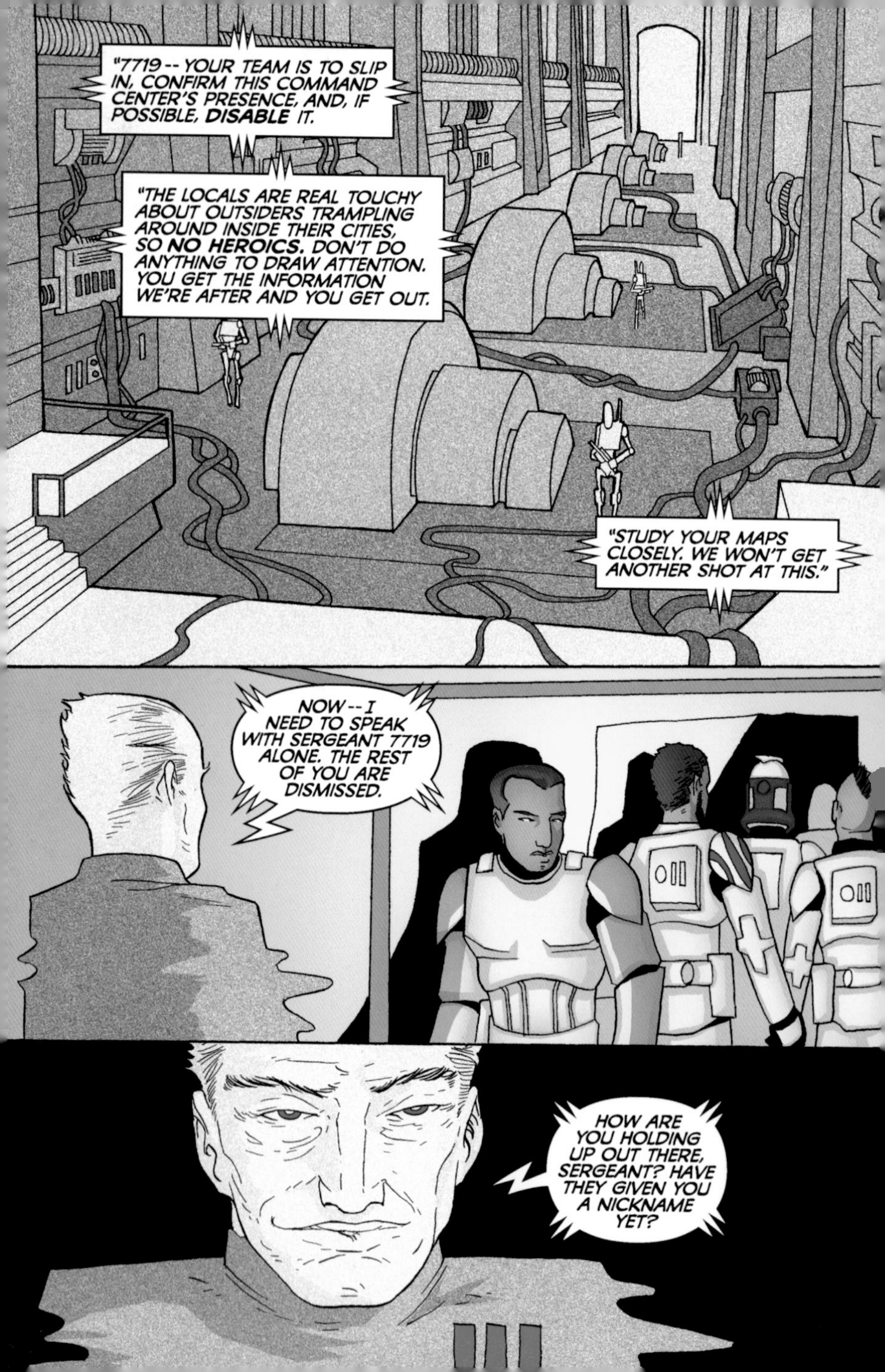
"7719 -- YOUR TEAM IS TO SLIP IN, CONFIRM THIS COMMAND CENTER'S PRESENCE, AND, IF POSSIBLE, DISABLE IT.
"THE LOCALS ARE REAL TOUCHY ABOUT OUTSIDERS TRAMPLING AROUND INSIDE THEIR CITIES, SO NO HEROICS. DON'T DO ANYTHING TO DRAW ATTENTION. YOU GET THE INFORMATION WE'RE AFTER AND YOU GET OUT.
"STUDY YOUR MAPS CLOSELY. WE WON'T GET ANOTHER SHOT AT THIS."
NOW -- I NEED TO SPEAK WITH SERGEANT 7719 ALONE. THE REST OF YOU ARE DISMISSED.
HOW ARE YOU HOLDING UP OUT THERE, SERGEANT? HAVE THEY GIVEN YOU A NICKNAME YET?

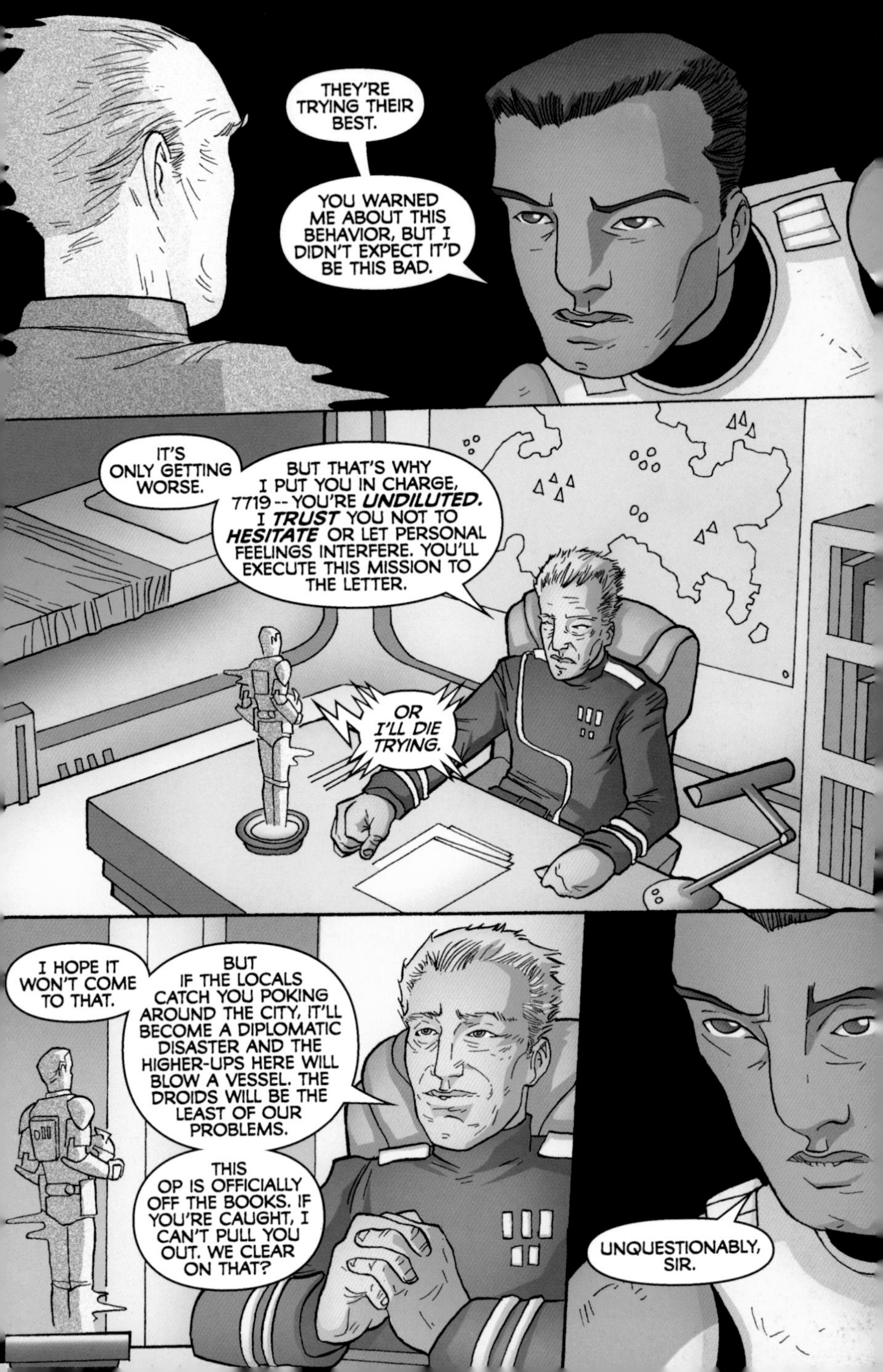

THEY'RE TRYING THEIR BEST.
YOU WARNED ME ABOUT THIS BEHAVIOR, BUT I DIDN'T EXPECT IT'D BE THIS BAD.
IT'S ONLY GETTING WORSE.
BUT THAT'S WHY I PUT YOU IN CHARGE, 7719 -- YOU'RE UNDILUTED. I TRUST YOU NOT TO HESITATE OR LET PERSONAL FEELINGS INTERFERE. YOU'LL EXECUTE THIS MISSION TO THE LETTER.
OR I'LL DIE TRYING.
I HOPE IT WON'T COME TO THAT.
BUT IF THE LOCALS CATCH YOU POKING AROUND THE CITY, IT'LL BECOME A DIPLOMATIC DISASTER AND THE HIGHER-UPS HERE WILL BLOW A VESSEL. THE DROIDS WILL BE THE LEAST OF OUR PROBLEMS.
THIS OP IS OFFICIALLY OFF THE BOOKS. IF YOU'RE CAUGHT, I CAN'T PULL YOU OUT. WE CLEAR ON THAT?
UNQUESTIONABLY, SIR.

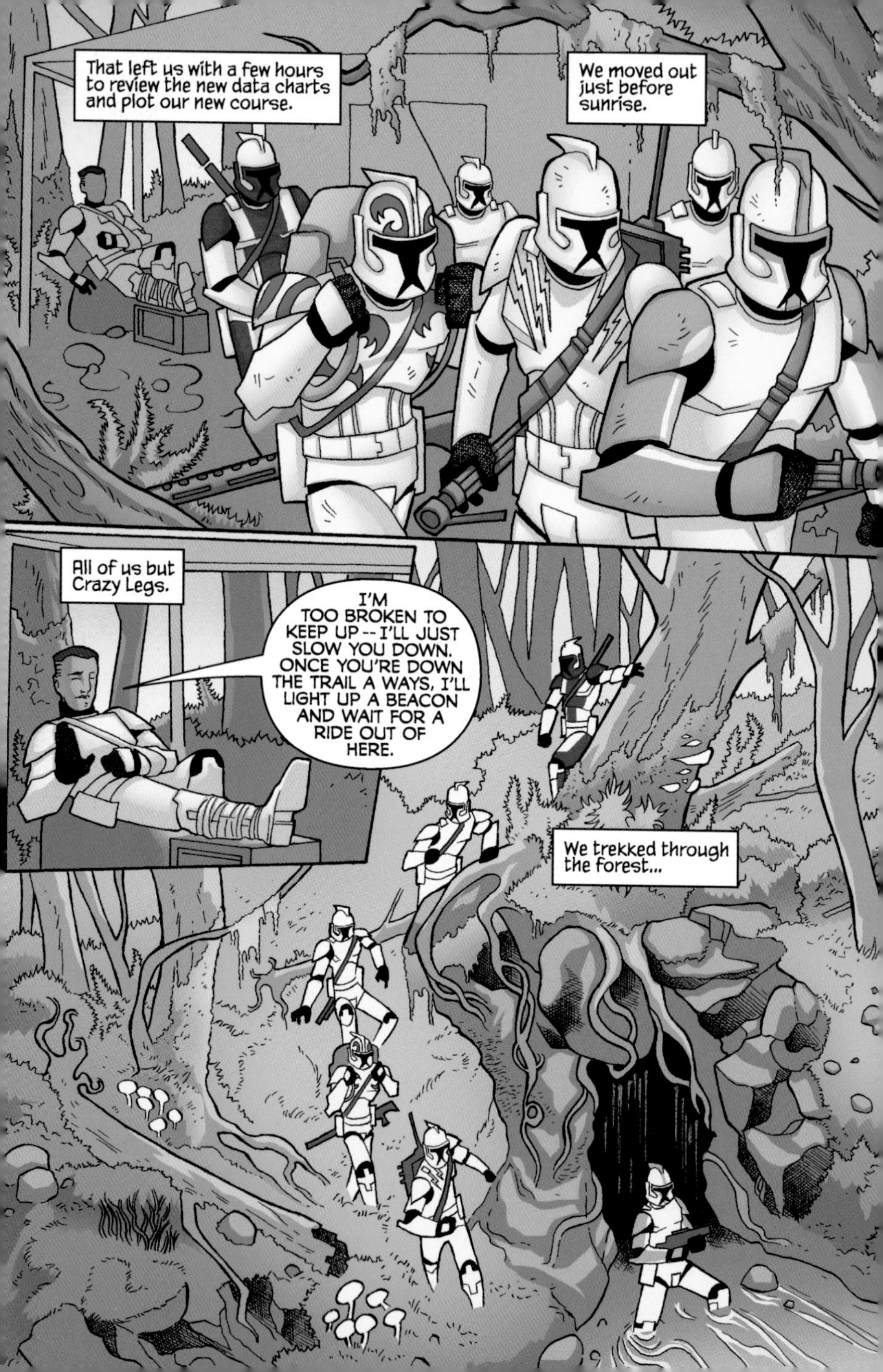
That left us with a few hours to review the new data charts and plot our new course.
We moved out just before sunrise.
All of us but Crazy Legs.
I'M TOO BROKEN TO KEEP UP -- I'LL JUST SLOW YOU DOWN. ONCE YOU'RE DOWN THE TRAIL A WAYS, I'LL LIGHT UP A BEACON AND WAIT FOR A RIDE OUT OF HERE.
We trekked through the forest...

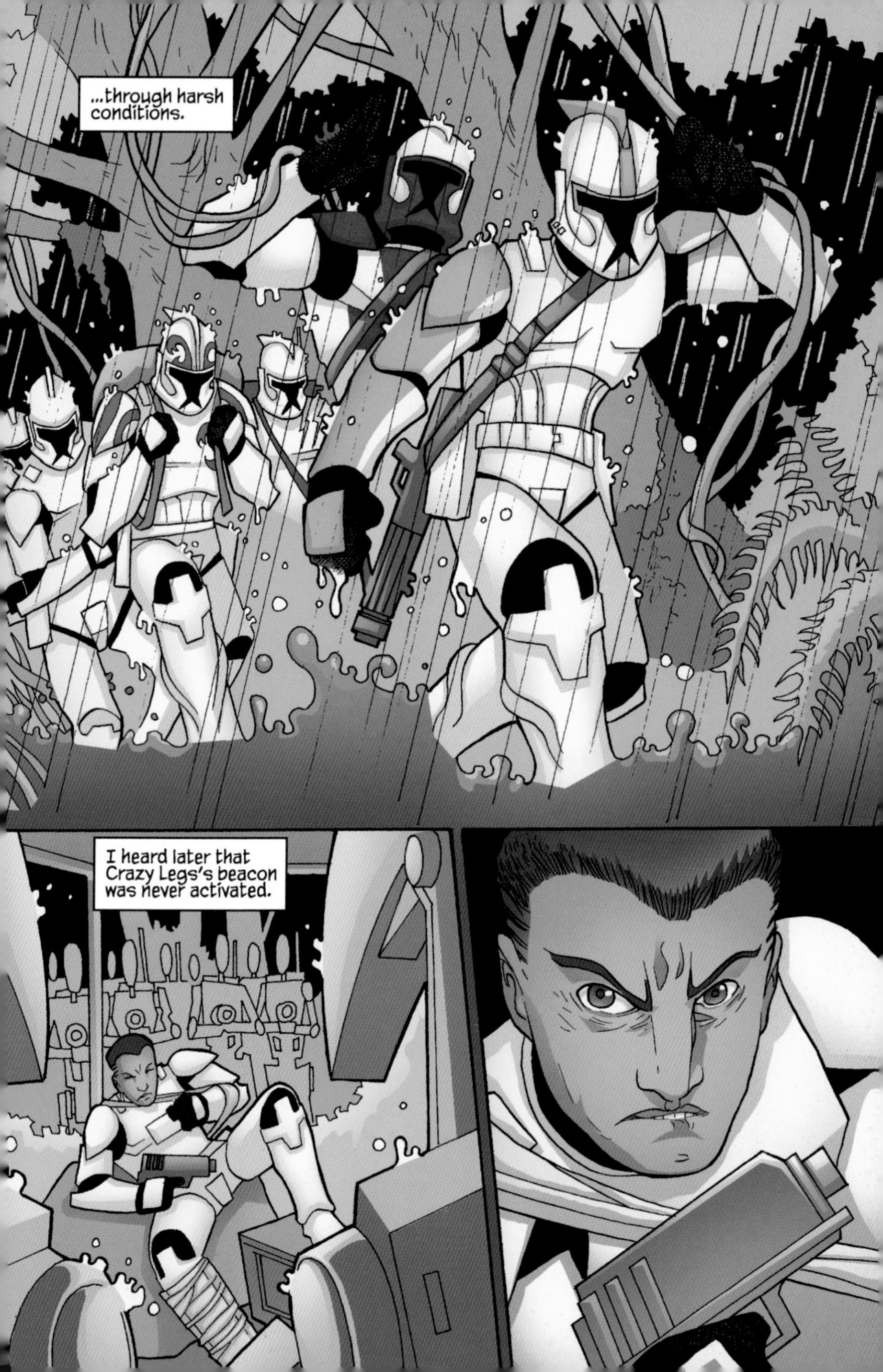
...through harsh conditions.
I heard later that Crazy Legs's beacon was never activated.

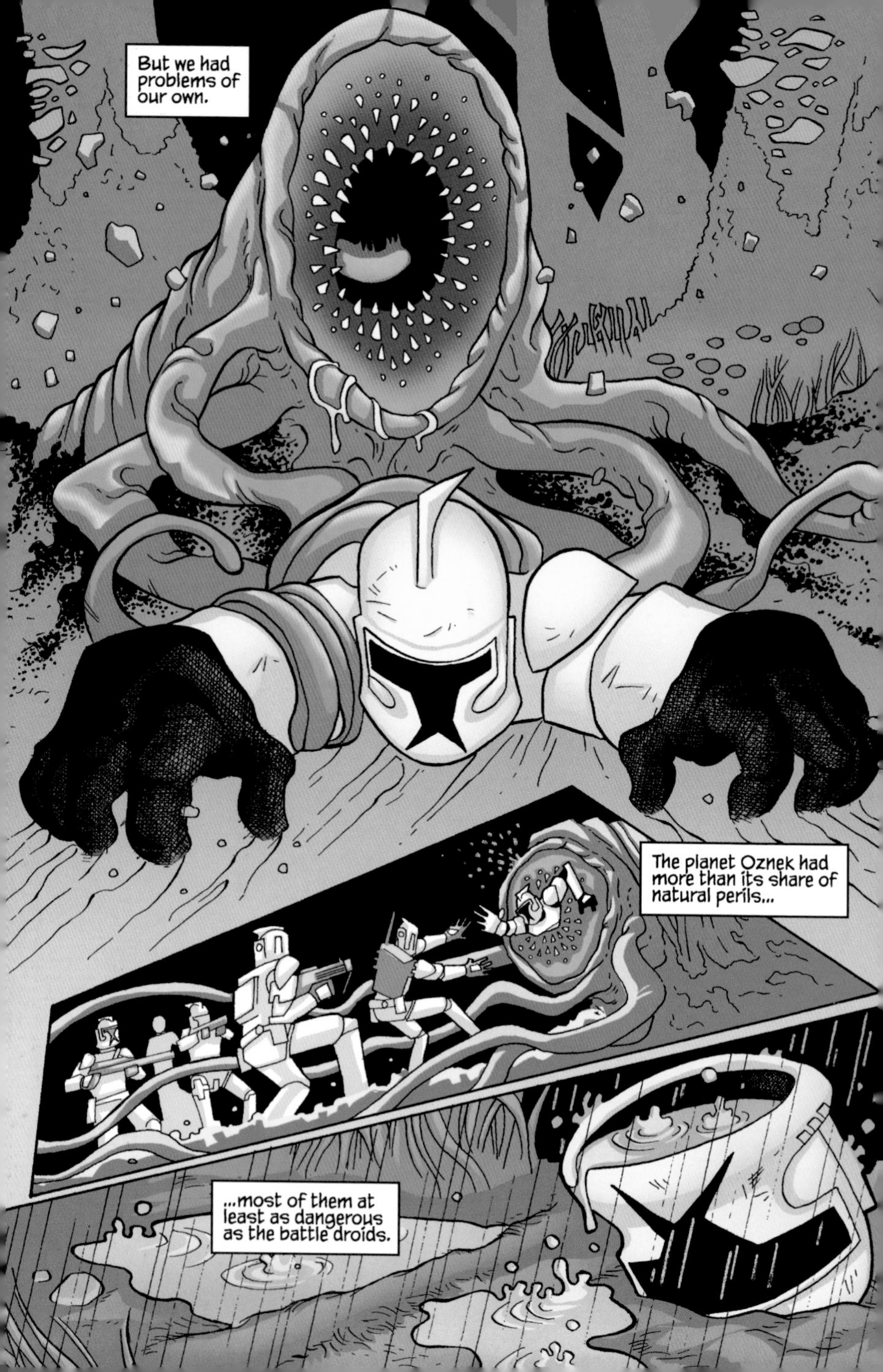

But we had problems of our own.
The planet Oznek had more than its share of natural perils...
...most of them at least as dangerous as the battle droids.

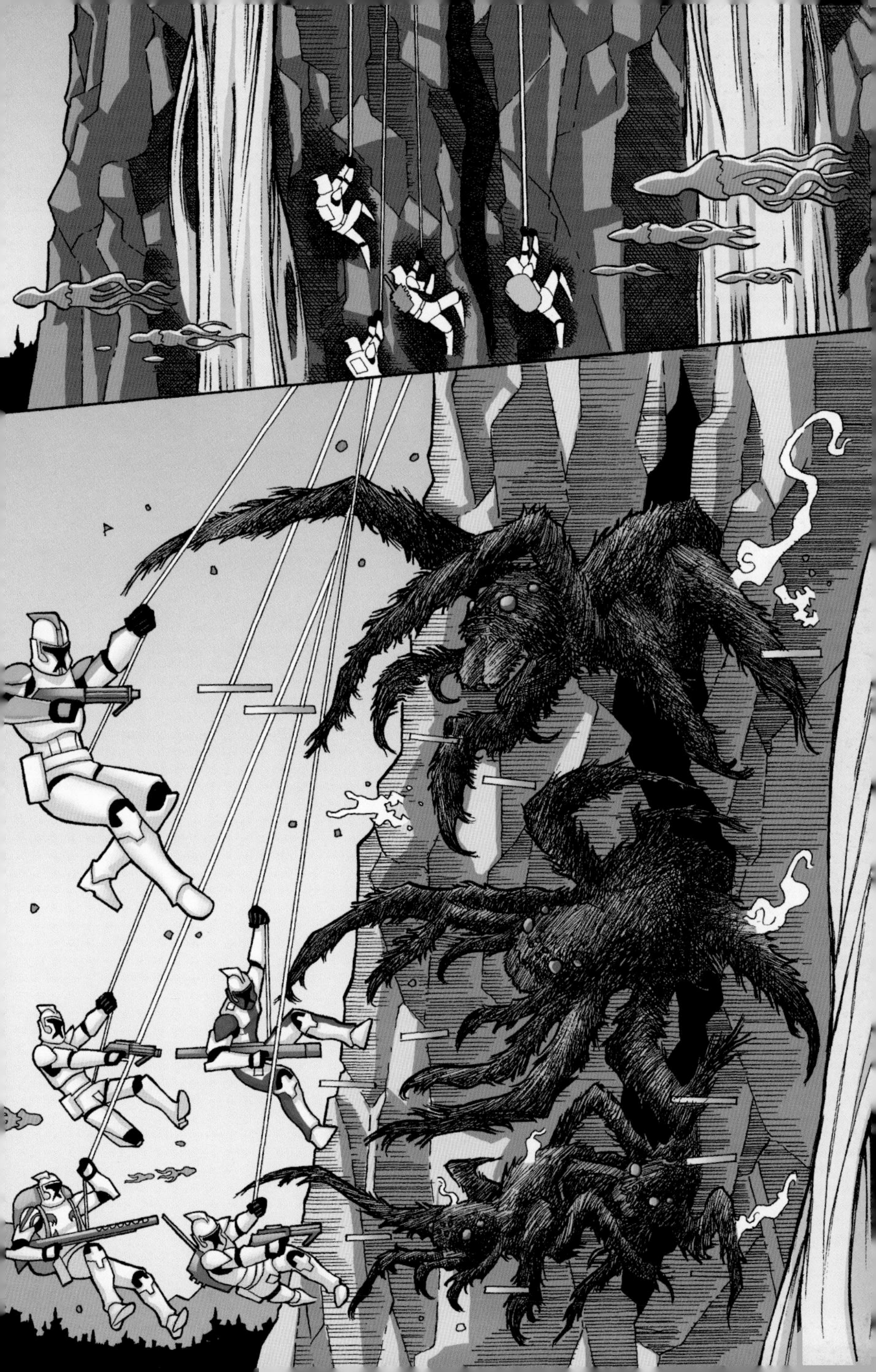

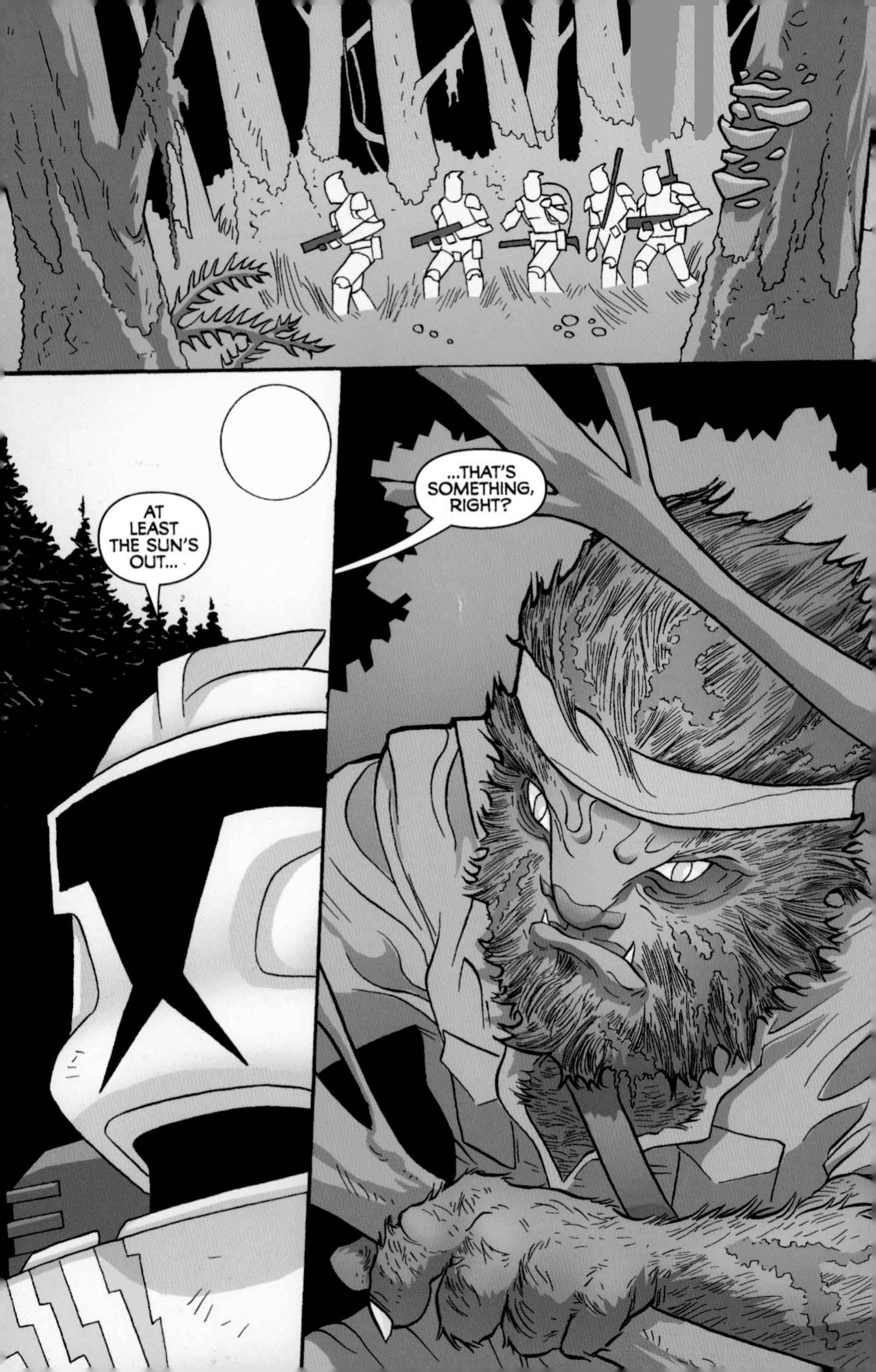
AT LEAST THE SUN'S OUT...
...THAT'S SOMETHING, RIGHT?

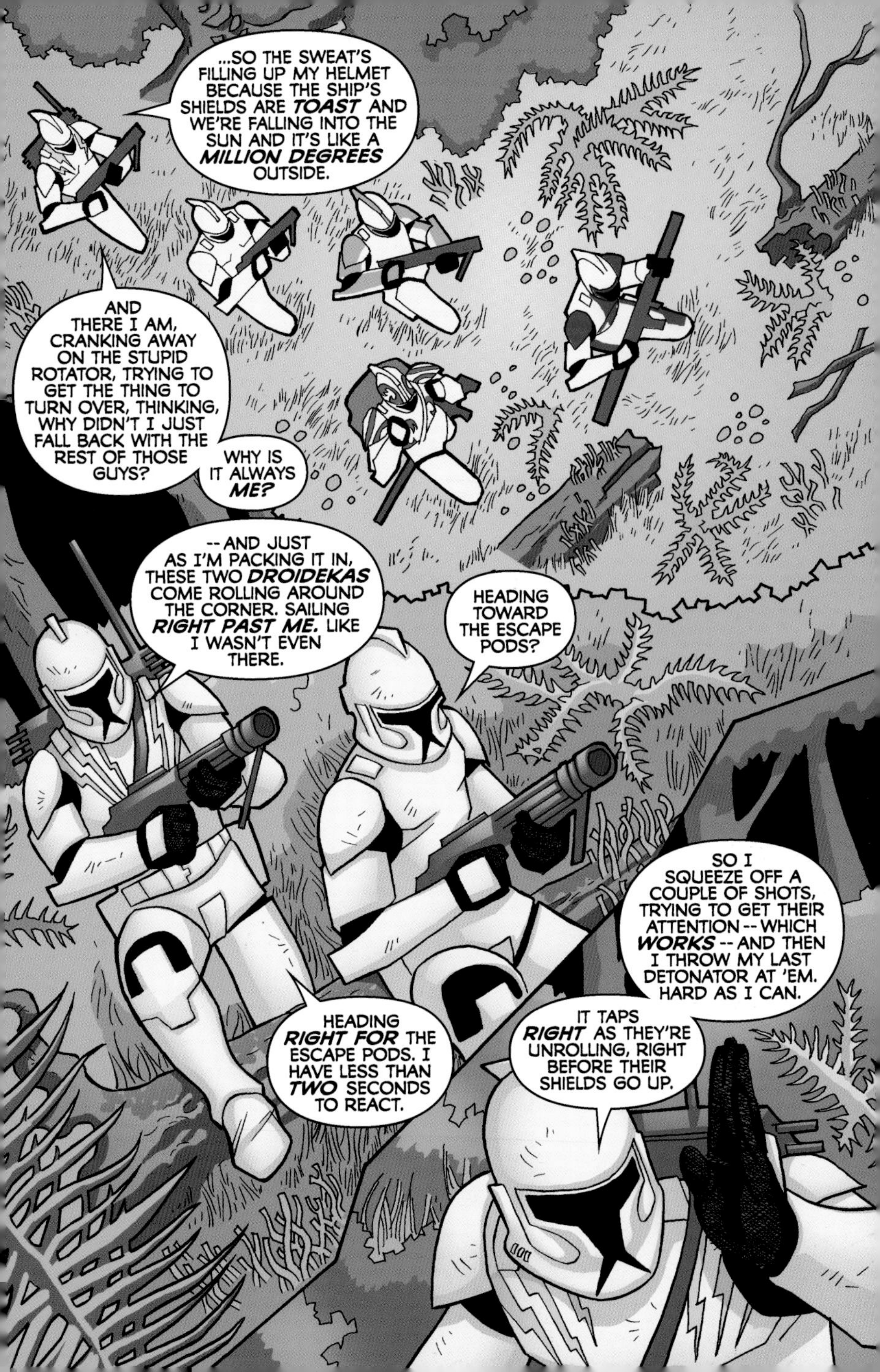
...SO THE SWEAT'S FILLING UP MY HELMET BECAUSE THE SHIP'S SHIELDS ARE *TOAST* AND WE'RE FALLING INTO THE SUN AND IT'S LIKE A *MILLION DEGREES* OUTSIDE.
AND THERE I AM, CRANKING AWAY ON THE STUPID ROTATOR, TRYING TO GET THE THING TO TURN OVER, THINKING, WHY DIDN'T I JUST FALL BACK WITH THE REST OF THOSE GUYS?
WHY IS IT ALWAYS *ME?*
--AND JUST AS I'M PACKING IT IN, THESE TWO *DROIDEKAS* COME ROLLING AROUND THE CORNER. SAILING *RIGHT PAST ME.* LIKE I WASN'T EVEN THERE.
HEADING TOWARD THE ESCAPE PODS?
HEADING *RIGHT FOR* THE ESCAPE PODS. I HAVE LESS THAN *TWO* SECONDS TO REACT.
SO I SQUEEZE OFF A COUPLE OF SHOTS, TRYING TO GET THEIR ATTENTION -- WHICH *WORKS* -- AND THEN I THROW MY LAST DETONATOR AT 'EM. HARD AS I CAN.
IT TAPS *RIGHT* AS THEY'RE UNROLLING, RIGHT BEFORE THEIR SHIELDS GO UP.

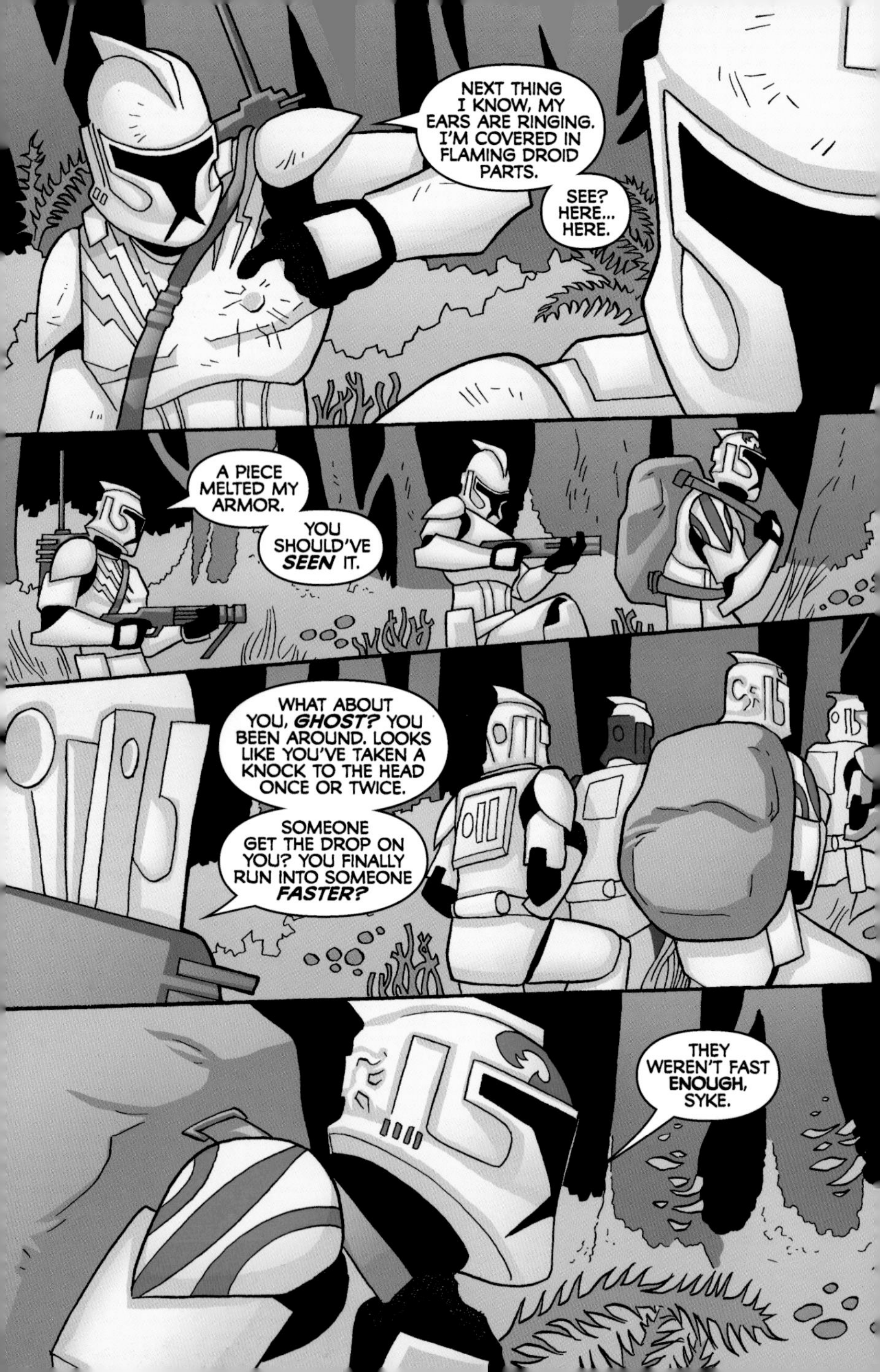
NEXT THING I KNOW, MY EARS ARE RINGING. I'M COVERED IN FLAMING DROID PARTS.
SEE? HERE... HERE.
A PIECE MELTED MY ARMOR.
YOU SHOULD'VE *SEEN* IT.
WHAT ABOUT YOU, *GHOST?* YOU BEEN AROUND. LOOKS LIKE YOU'VE TAKEN A KNOCK TO THE HEAD ONCE OR TWICE.
SOMEONE GET THE DROP ON YOU? YOU FINALLY RUN INTO SOMEONE *FASTER?*
THEY WEREN'T FAST **ENOUGH,** SYKE.

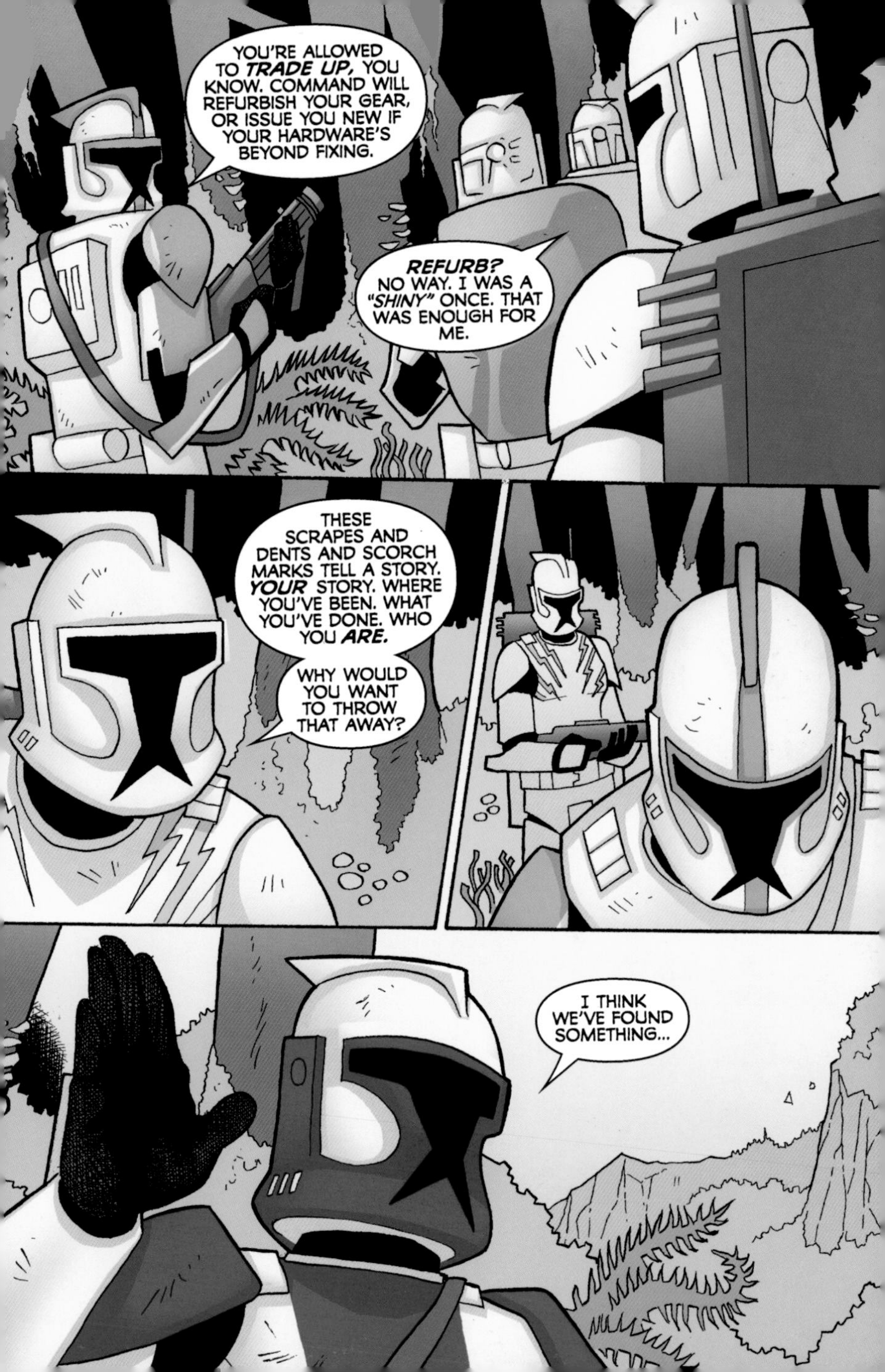
YOU'RE ALLOWED TO *TRADE UP*, YOU KNOW. COMMAND WILL REFURBISH YOUR GEAR, OR ISSUE YOU NEW IF YOUR HARDWARE'S BEYOND FIXING.
REFURB? NO WAY. I WAS A *"SHINY"* ONCE. THAT WAS ENOUGH FOR ME.
THESE SCRAPES AND DENTS AND SCORCH MARKS TELL A STORY. *YOUR* STORY. WHERE YOU'VE BEEN. WHAT YOU'VE DONE. WHO YOU *ARE.*
WHY WOULD YOU WANT TO THROW THAT AWAY?
I THINK WE'VE FOUND SOMETHING...

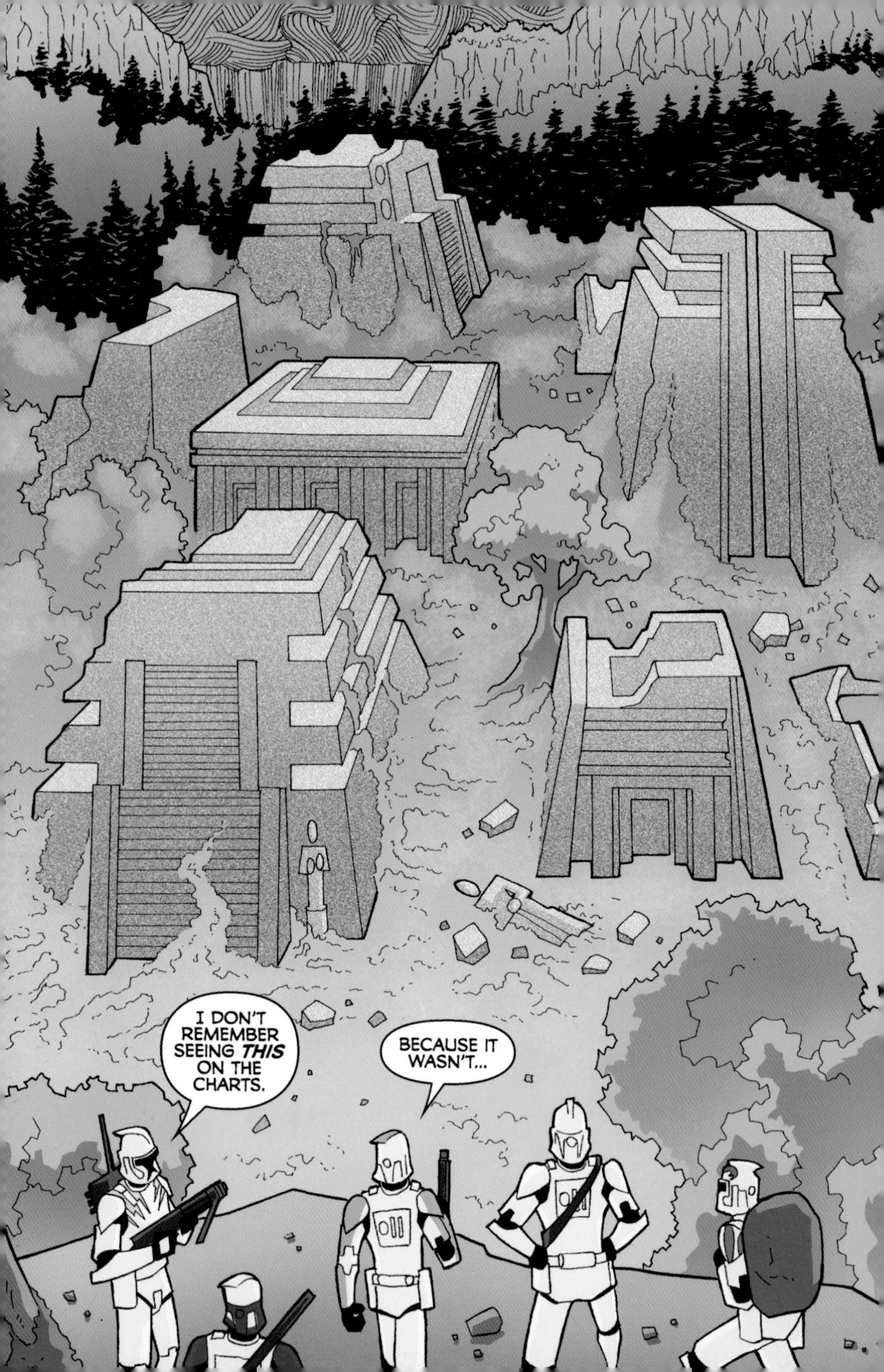
I DON'T REMEMBER SEEING *THIS* ON THE CHARTS.
BECAUSE IT WASN'T...

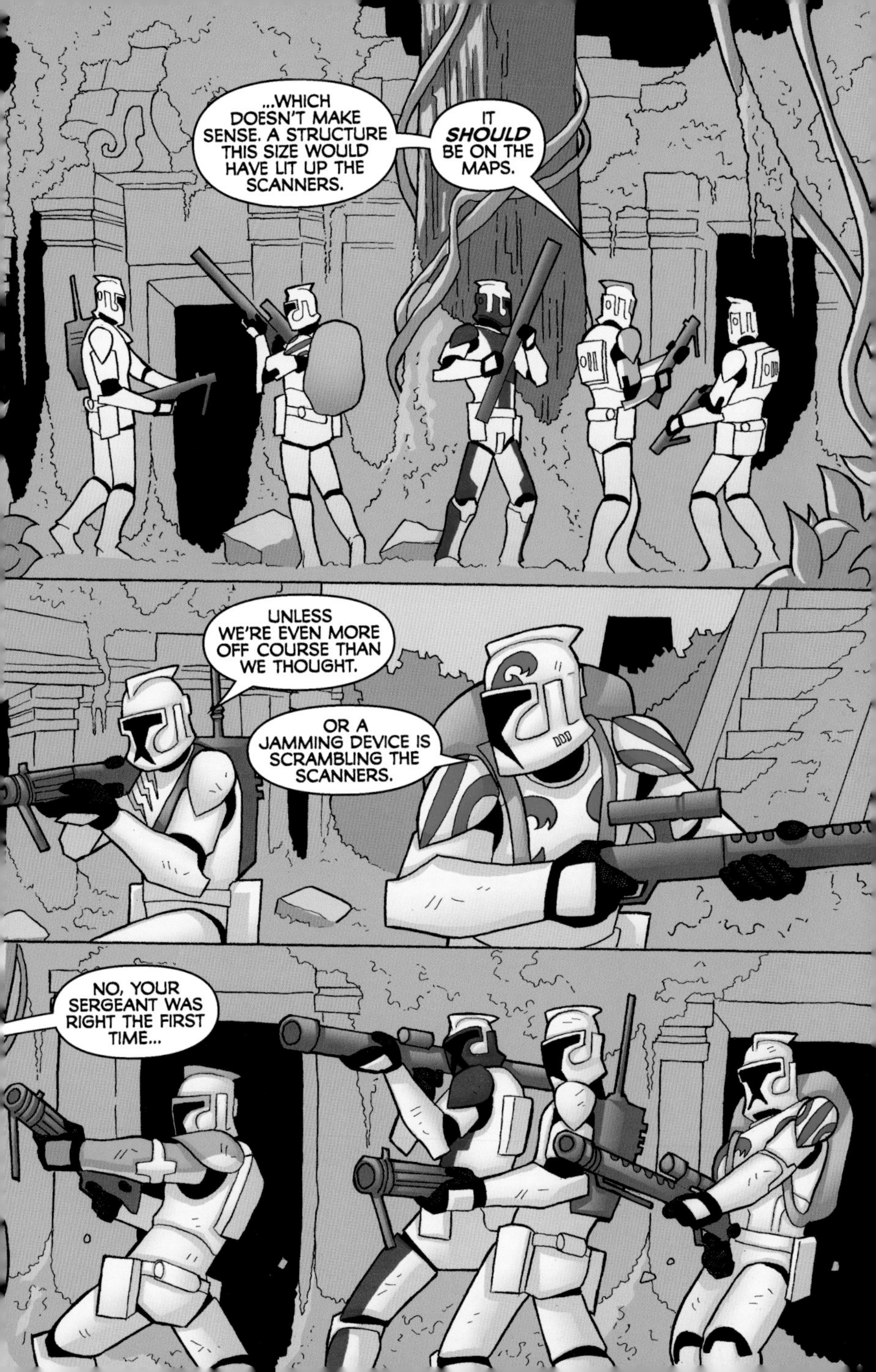
...WHICH DOESN'T MAKE SENSE. A STRUCTURE THIS SIZE WOULD HAVE LIT UP THE SCANNERS.
IT *SHOULD* BE ON THE MAPS.
UNLESS WE'RE EVEN MORE OFF COURSE THAN WE THOUGHT.
OR A JAMMING DEVICE IS SCRAMBLING THE SCANNERS.
NO, YOUR SERGEANT WAS RIGHT THE FIRST TIME...

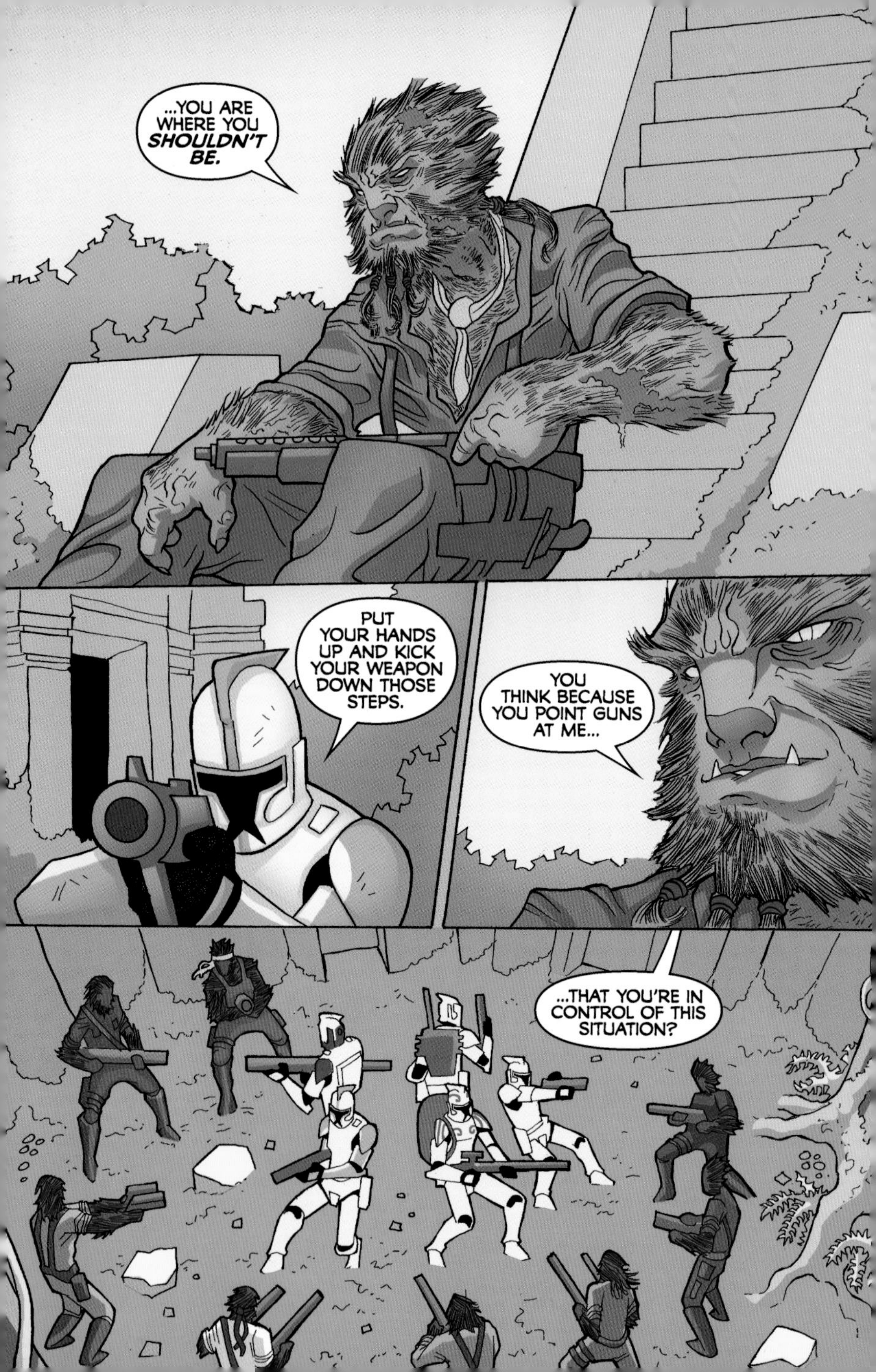
...YOU ARE WHERE YOU SHOULDN'T BE.
PUT YOUR HANDS UP AND KICK YOUR WEAPON DOWN THOSE STEPS.
YOU THINK BECAUSE YOU POINT GUNS AT ME...
...THAT YOU'RE IN CONTROL OF THIS SITUATION?

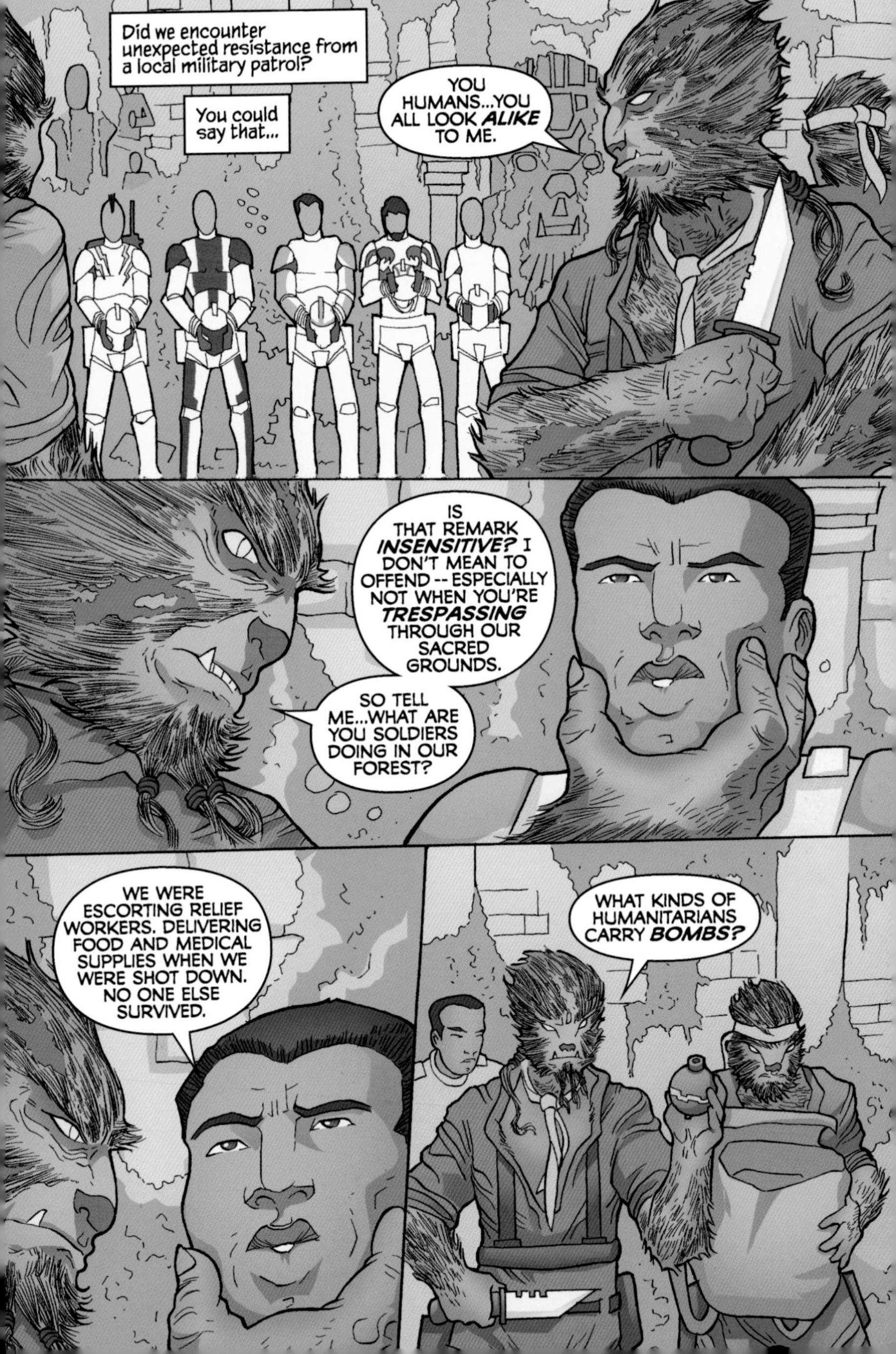
Did we encounter unexpected resistance from a local military patrol?
You could say that...
YOU HUMANS...YOU ALL LOOK *ALIKE* TO ME.
IS THAT REMARK *INSENSITIVE?* I DON'T MEAN TO OFFEND -- ESPECIALLY NOT WHEN YOU'RE *TRESPASSING* THROUGH OUR SACRED GROUNDS.
SO TELL ME...WHAT ARE YOU SOLDIERS DOING IN OUR FOREST?
WE WERE ESCORTING RELIEF WORKERS. DELIVERING FOOD AND MEDICAL SUPPLIES WHEN WE WERE SHOT DOWN. NO ONE ELSE SURVIVED.
WHAT KINDS OF HUMANITARIANS CARRY *BOMBS?*

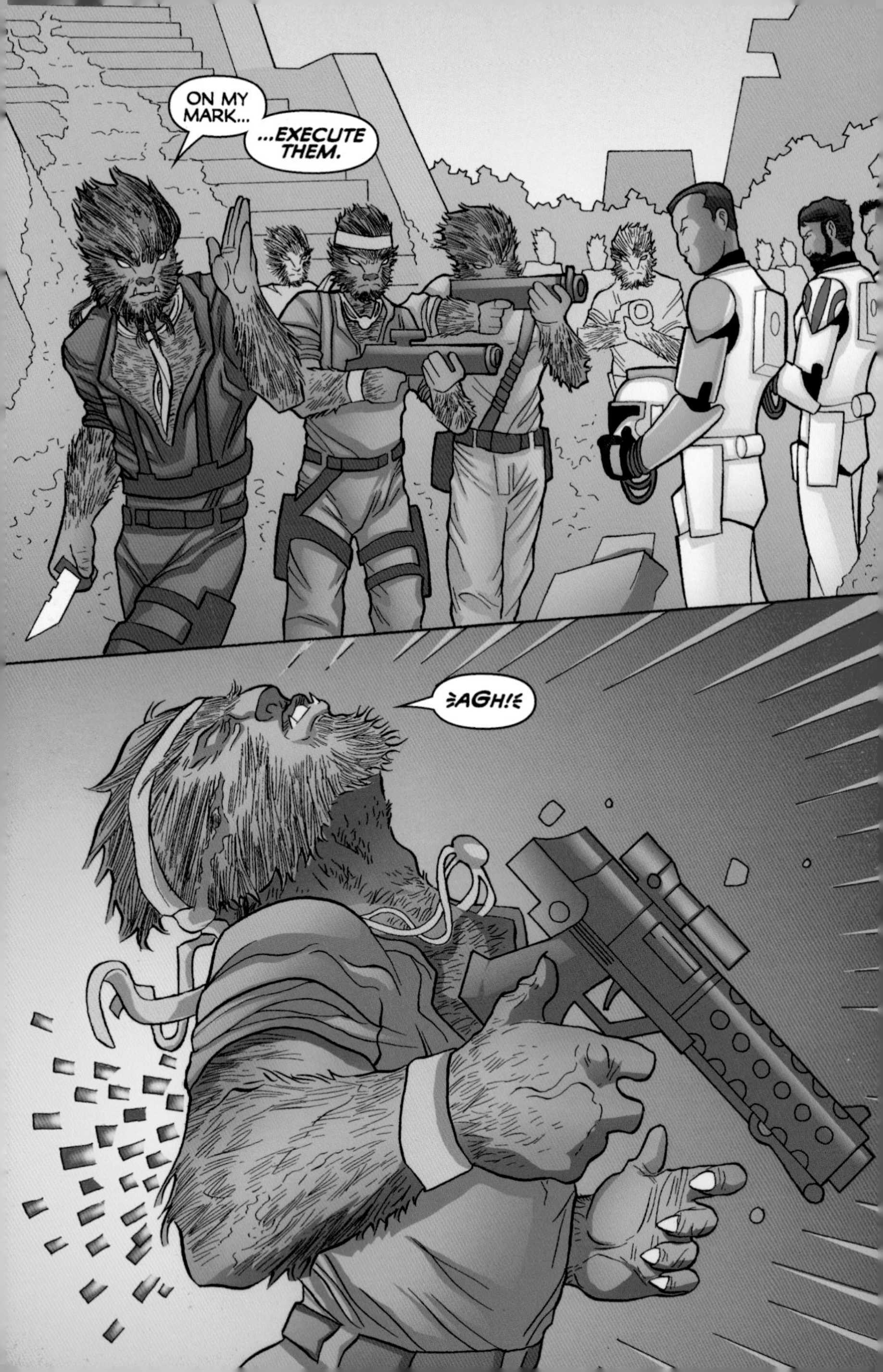
ON MY MARK...
...EXECUTE THEM.
AGH!

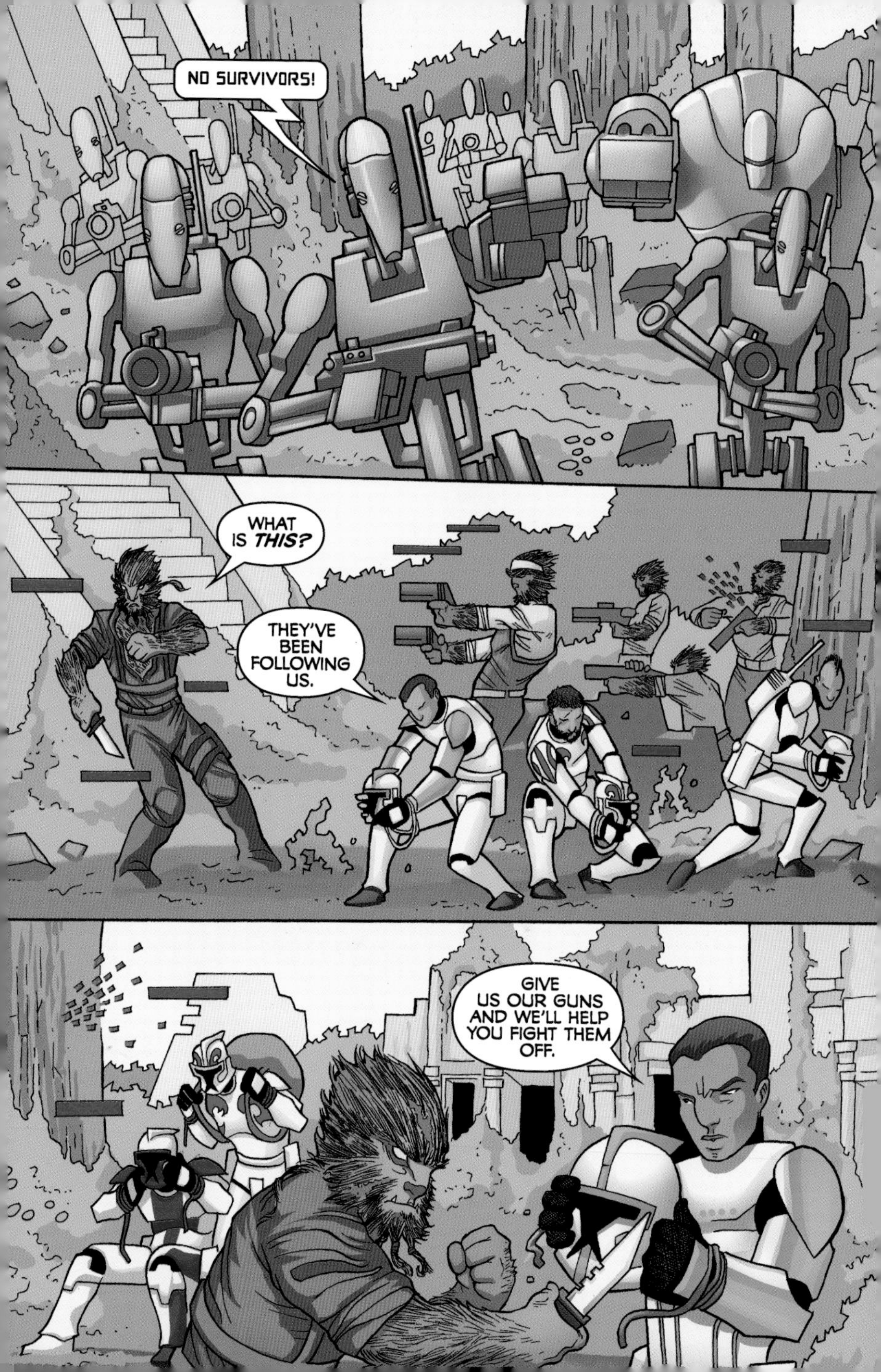
NO SURVIVORS!
WHAT IS *THIS?*
THEY'VE BEEN FOLLOWING US.
GIVE US OUR GUNS AND WE'LL HELP YOU FIGHT THEM OFF.

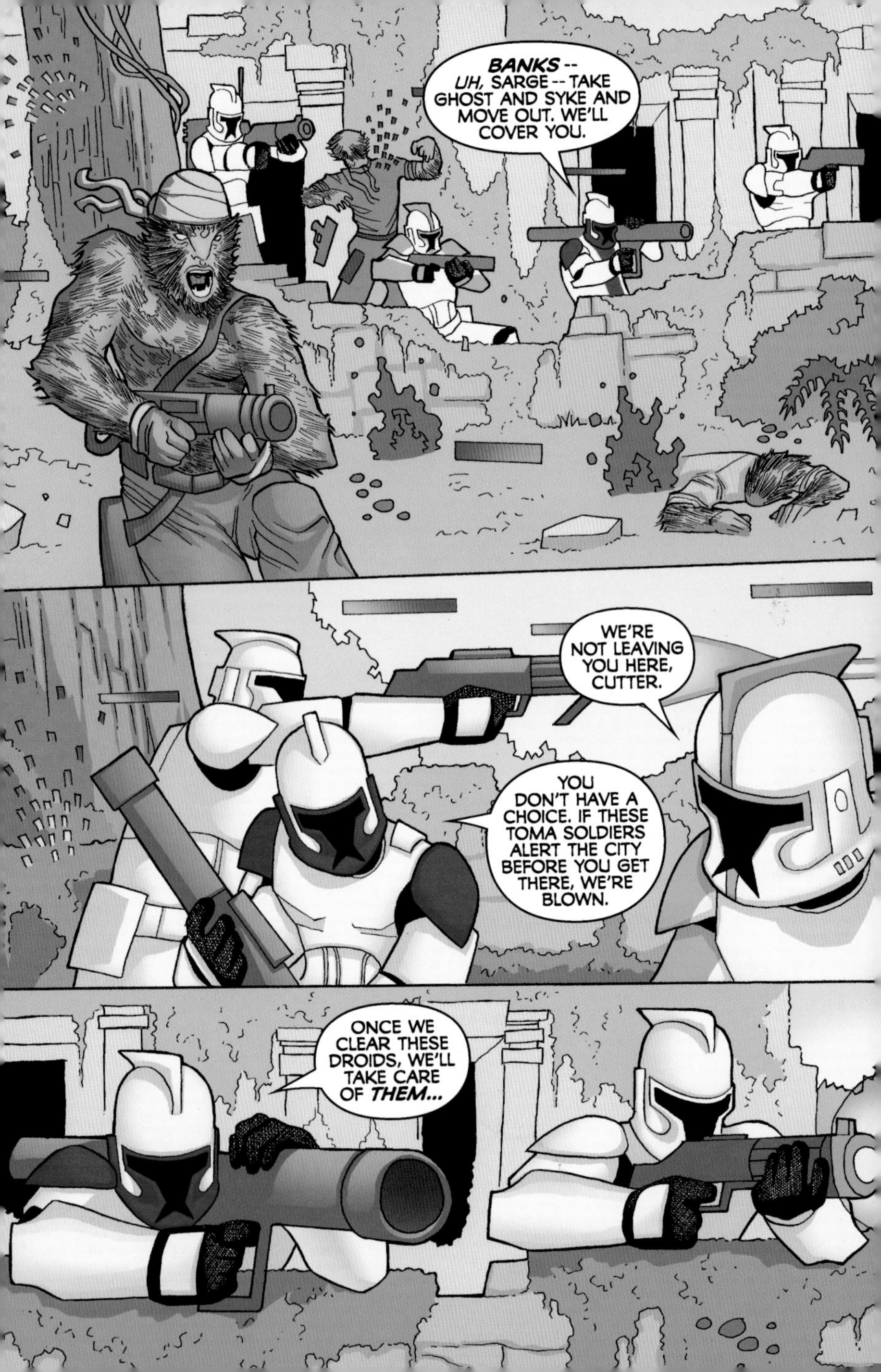
BANKS -- UH, SARGE -- TAKE GHOST AND SYKE AND MOVE OUT. WE'LL COVER YOU.
WE'RE NOT LEAVING YOU HERE, CUTTER.
YOU DON'T HAVE A CHOICE. IF THESE TOMA SOLDIERS ALERT THE CITY BEFORE YOU GET THERE, WE'RE BLOWN.
ONCE WE CLEAR THESE DROIDS, WE'LL TAKE CARE OF THEM...

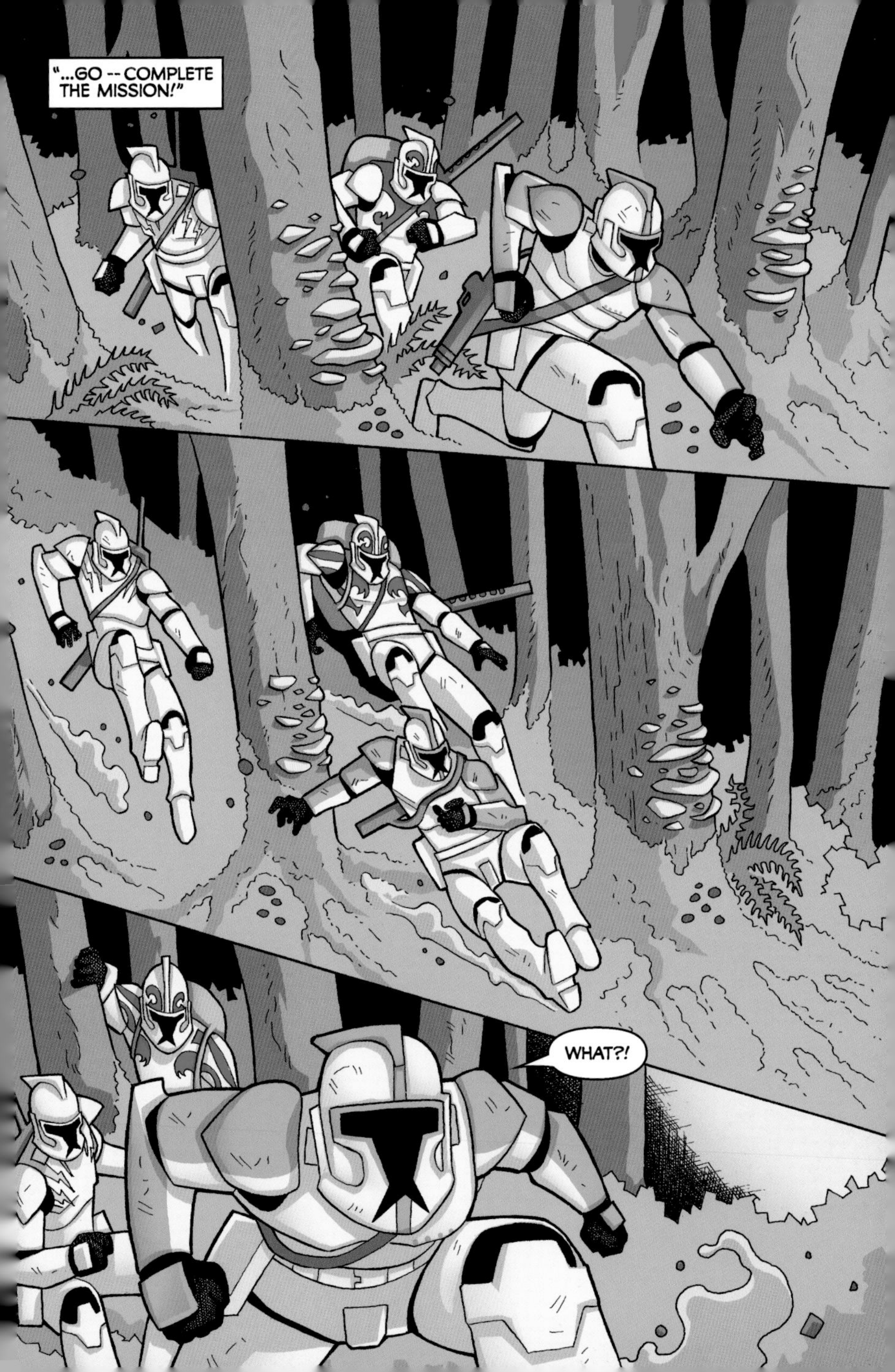
"...GO -- COMPLETE THE MISSION!"
WHAT?!

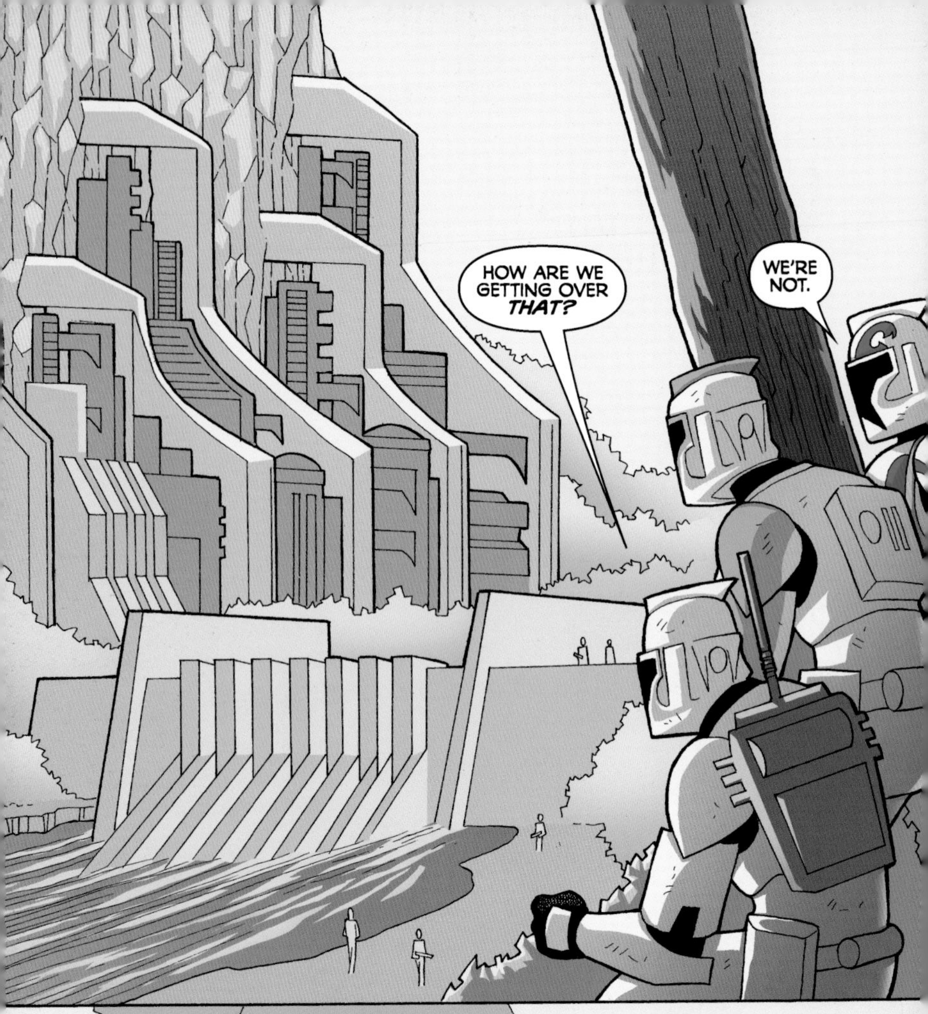
HOW ARE WE GETTING OVER *THAT?*
WE'RE NOT.
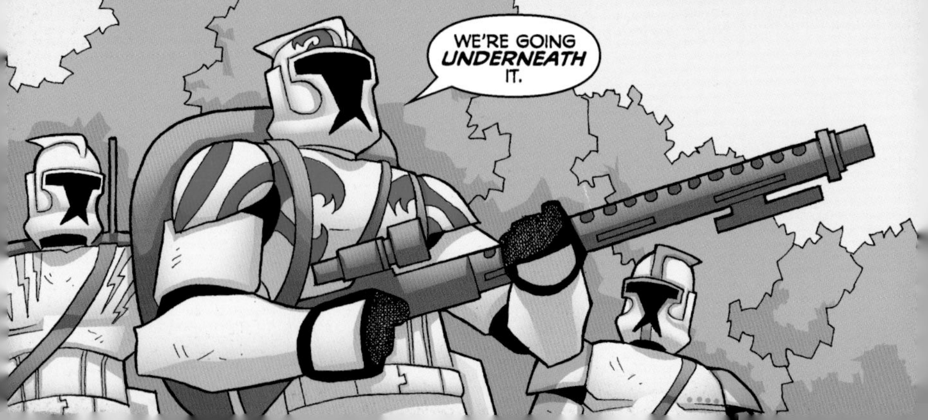
WE'RE GOING *UNDERNEATH* IT.

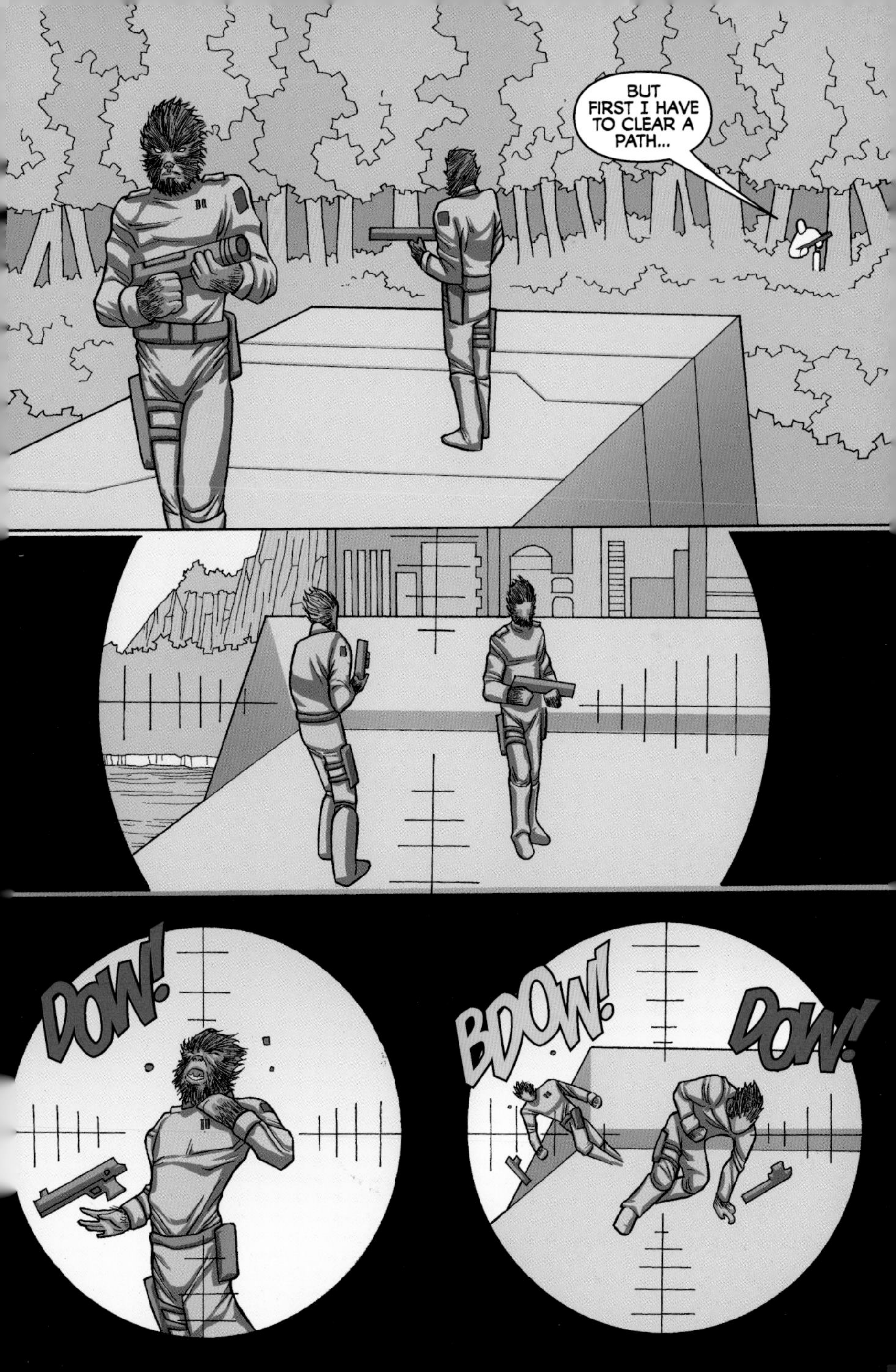
BUT FIRST I HAVE TO CLEAR A PATH...
DOW!
BDOW!
DOW!

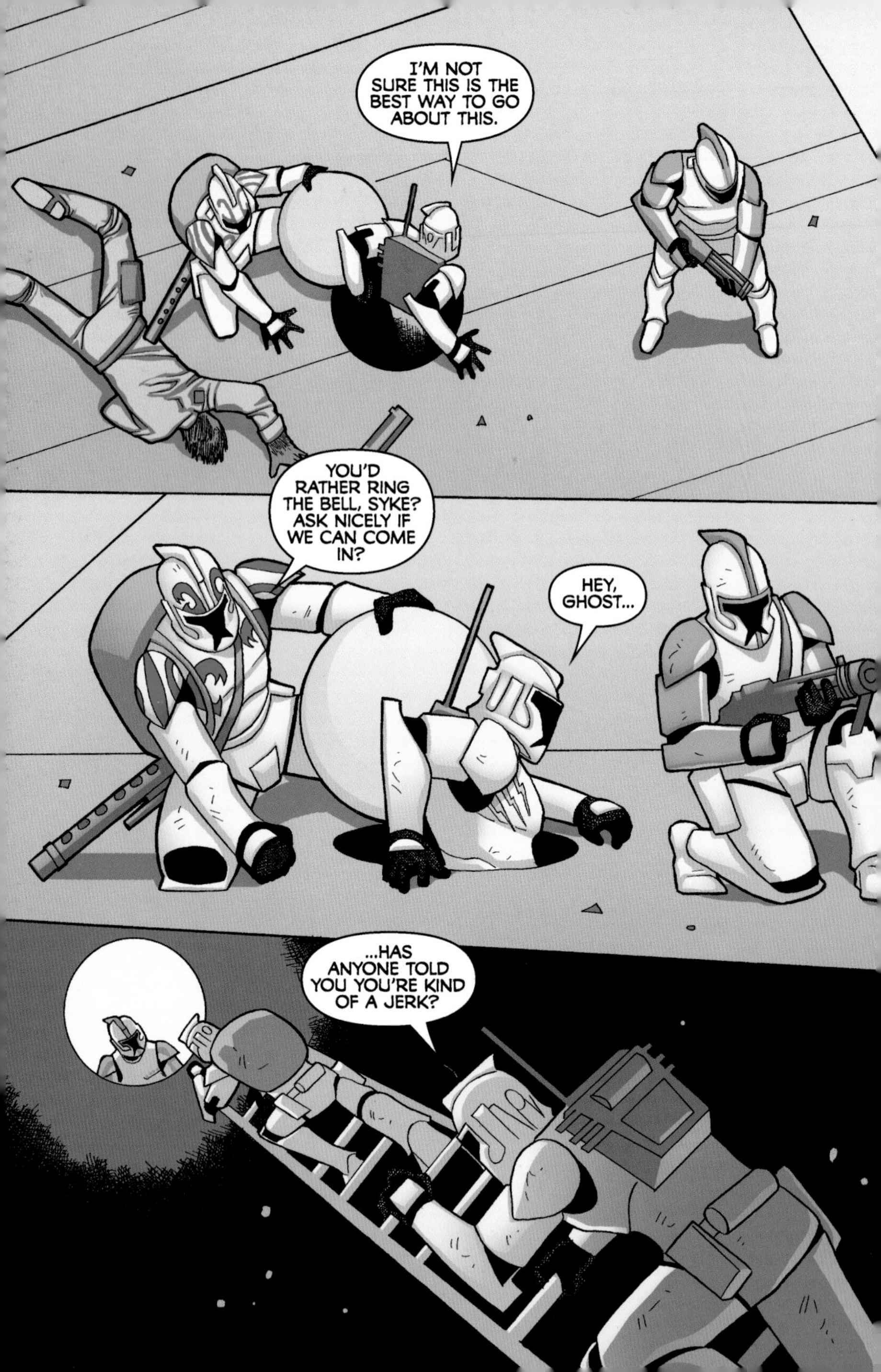
I'M NOT SURE THIS IS THE BEST WAY TO GO ABOUT THIS.
YOU'D RATHER RING THE BELL, SYKE? ASK NICELY IF WE CAN COME IN?
HEY, GHOST...
...HAS ANYONE TOLD YOU YOU'RE KIND OF A JERK?

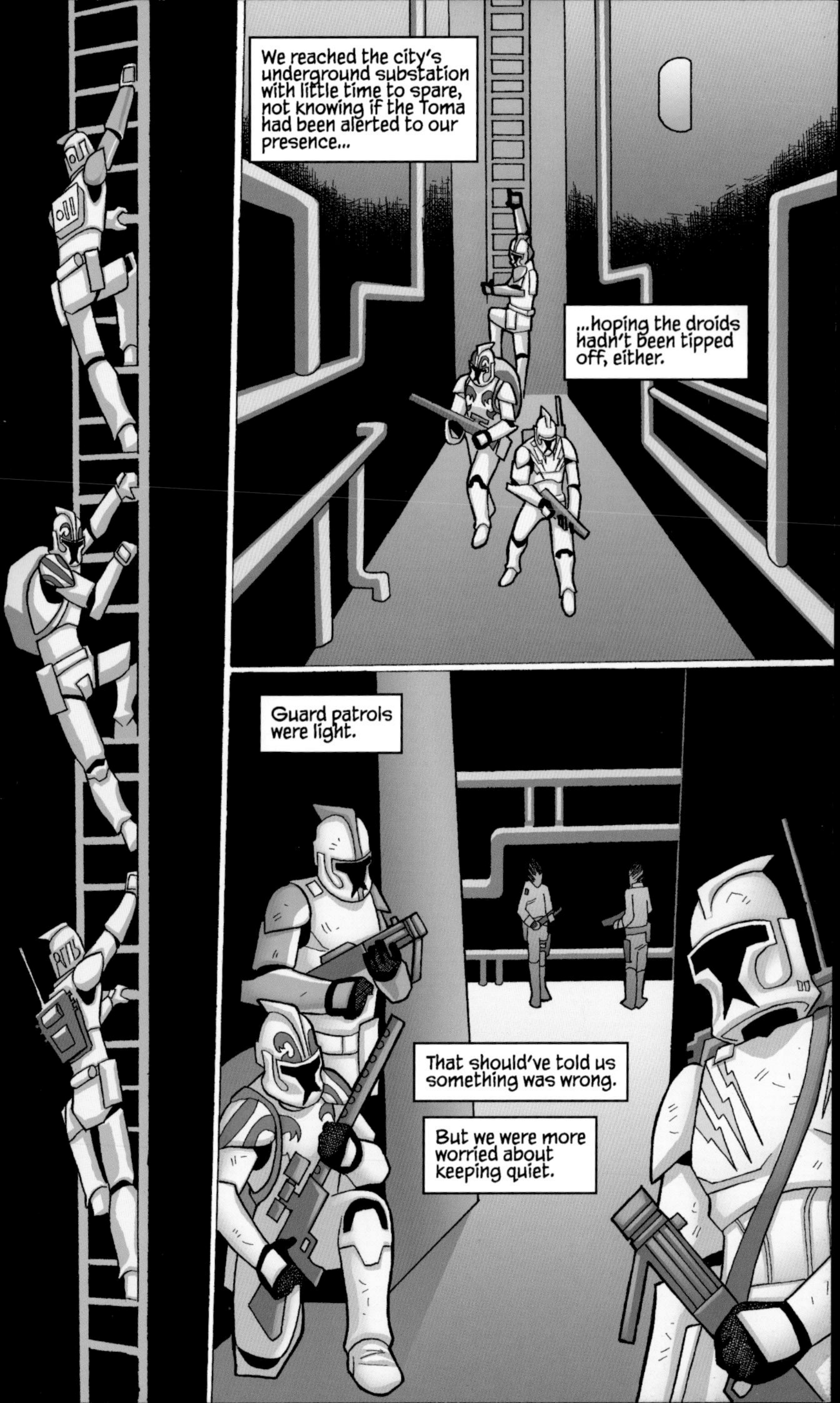
We reached the city's underground substation with little time to spare, not knowing if the Toma had been alerted to our presence...
...hoping the droids hadn't been tipped off, either.
Guard patrols were light.
That should've told us something was wrong.
But we were more worried about keeping quiet.

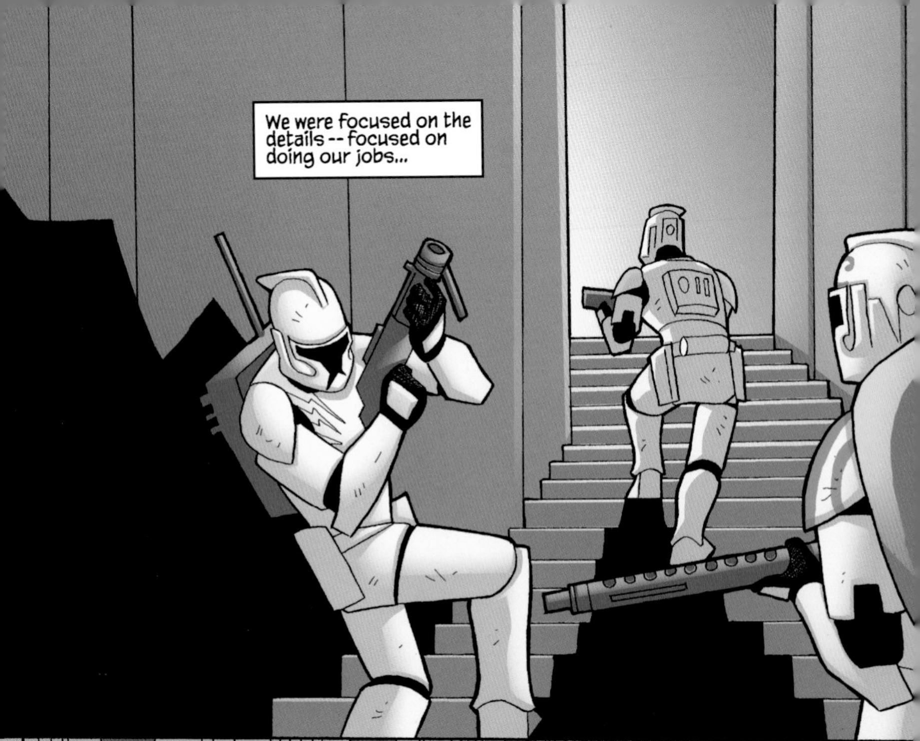
We were focused on the details -- focused on doing our jobs...

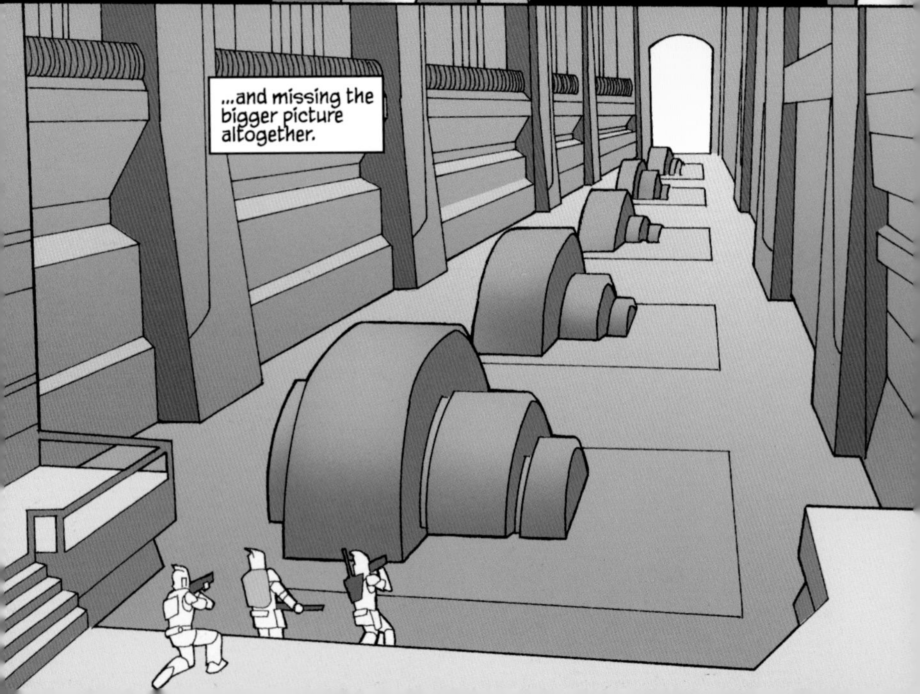
...and missing the bigger picture altogether.

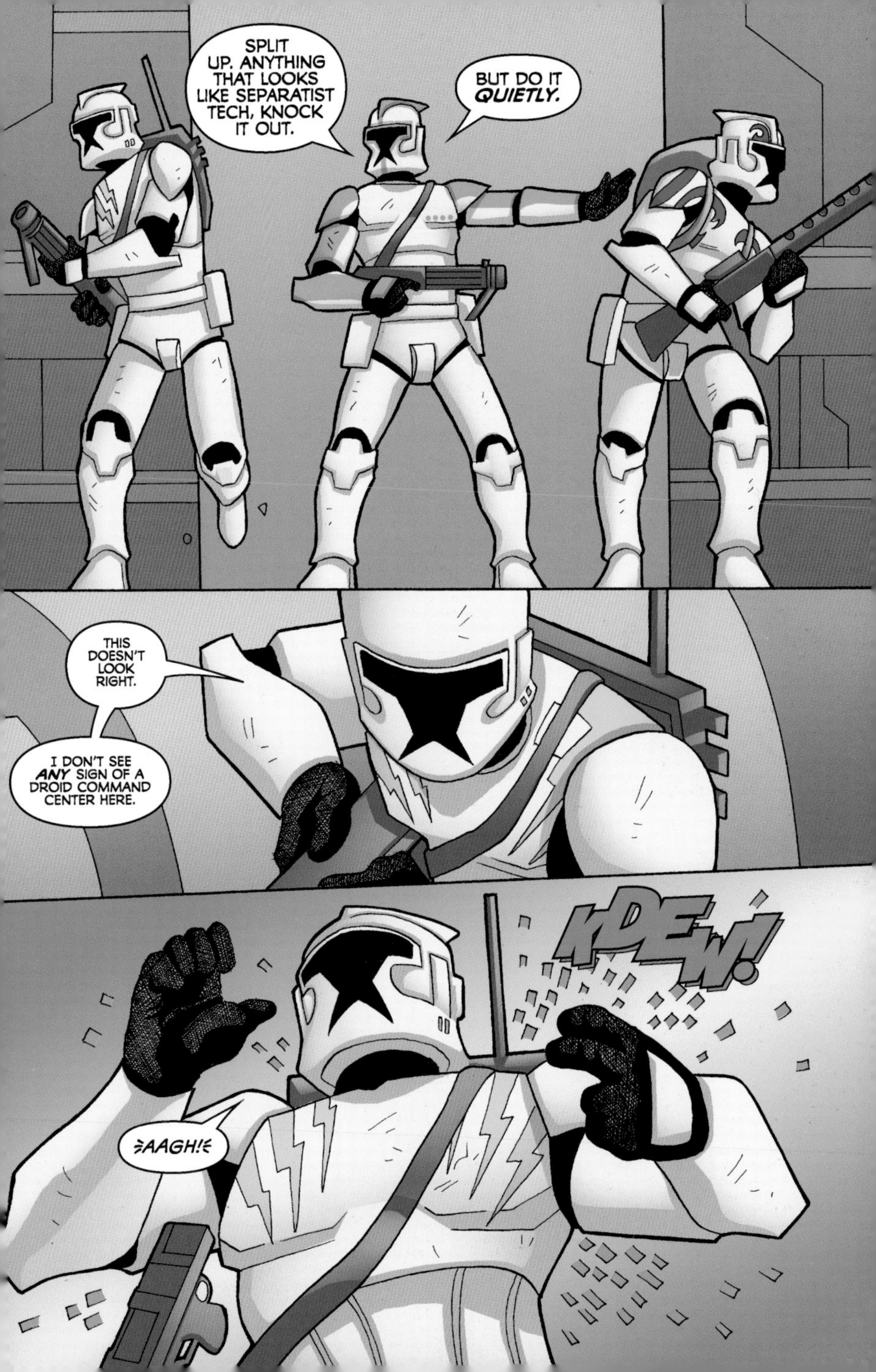
SPLIT UP. ANYTHING THAT LOOKS LIKE SEPARATIST TECH, KNOCK IT OUT.
BUT DO IT *QUIETLY.*
THIS DOESN'T LOOK RIGHT.
I DON'T SEE *ANY* SIGN OF A DROID COMMAND CENTER HERE.
KDEW!
AAGH!

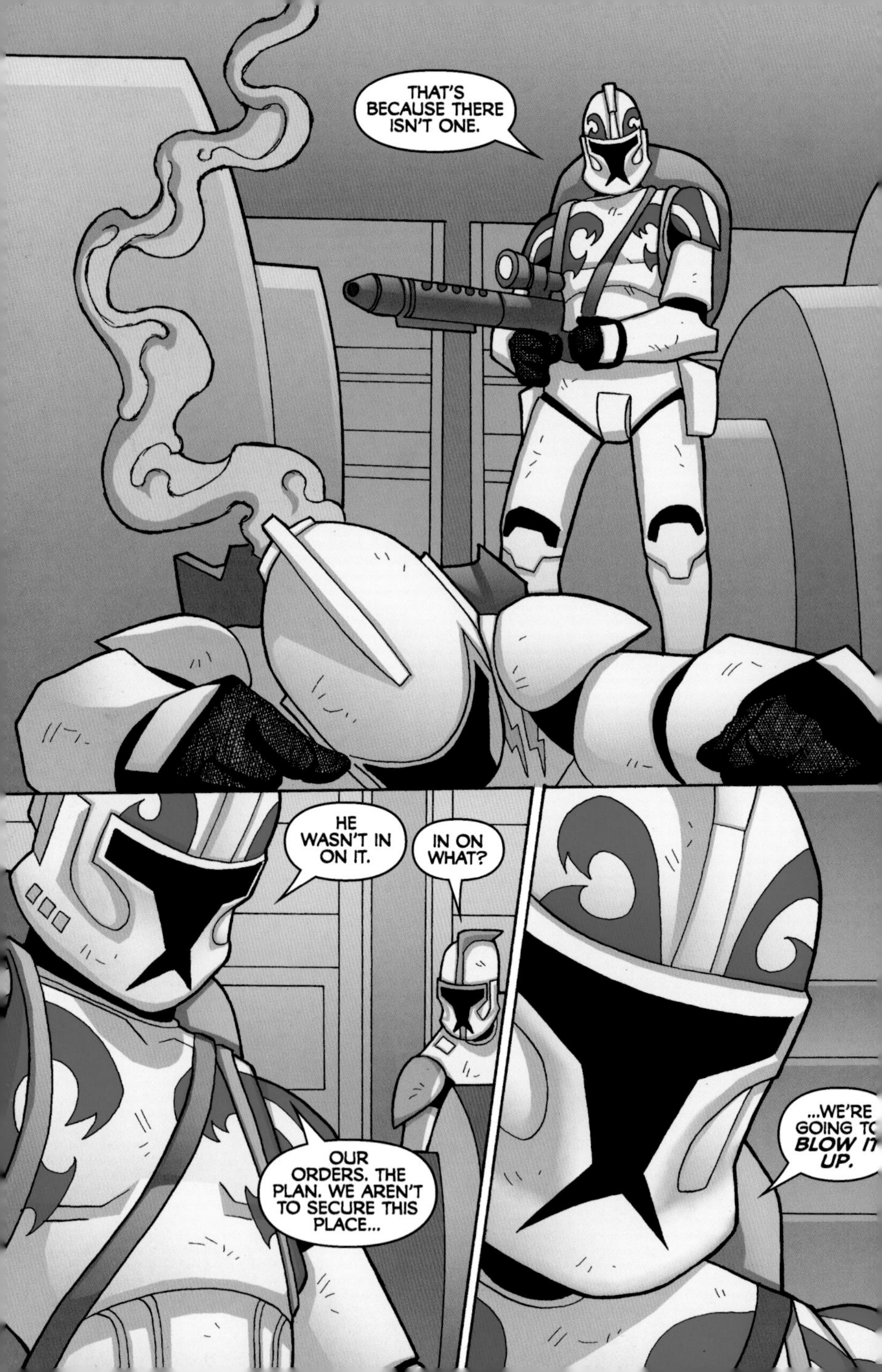
THAT'S BECAUSE THERE ISN'T ONE.
HE WASN'T IN ON IT.
IN ON WHAT?
OUR ORDERS. THE PLAN. WE AREN'T TO SECURE THIS PLACE...
...WE'RE GOING TO *BLOW IT UP.*

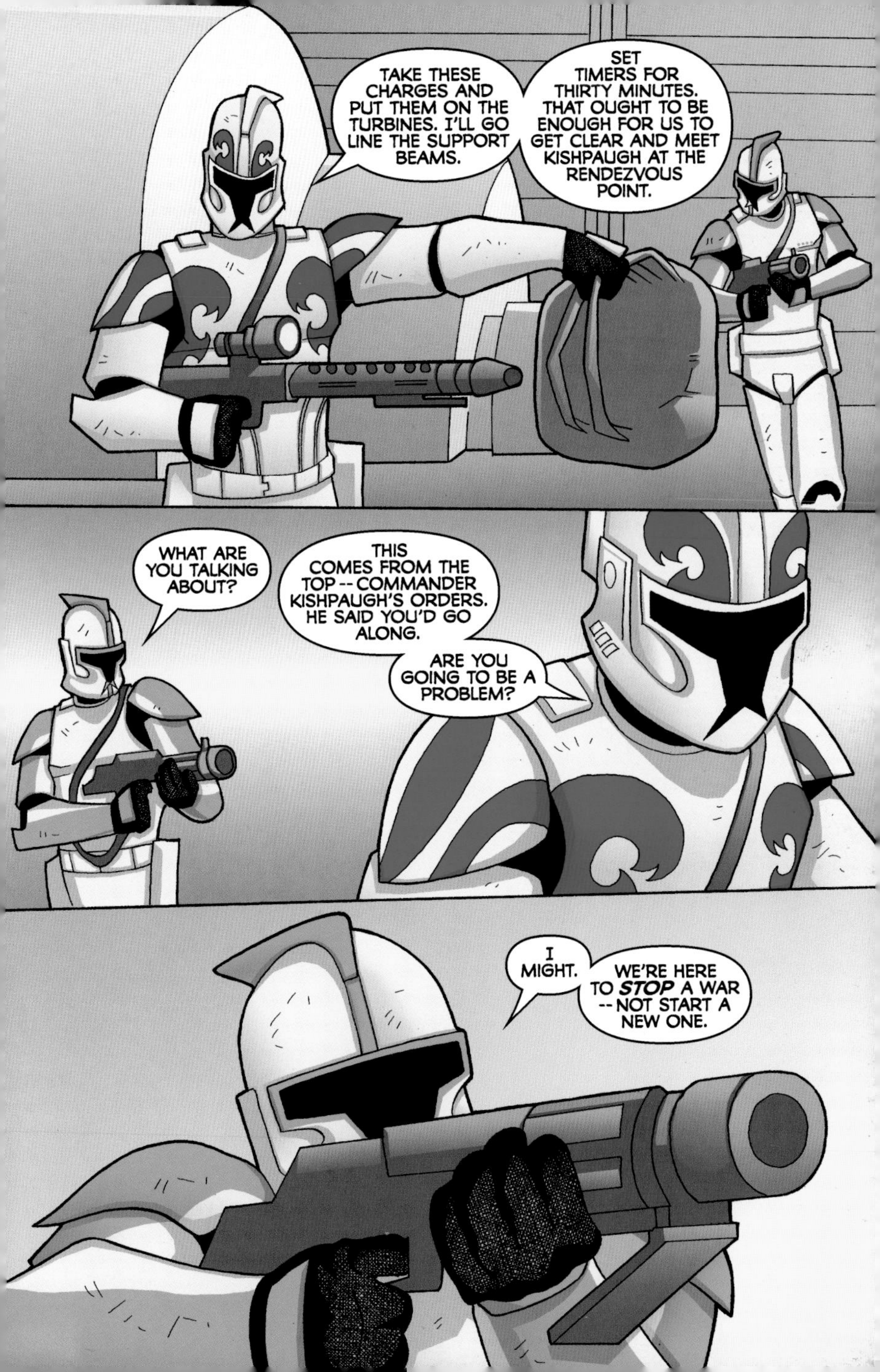
TAKE THESE CHARGES AND PUT THEM ON THE TURBINES. I'LL GO LINE THE SUPPORT BEAMS.
SET TIMERS FOR THIRTY MINUTES. THAT OUGHT TO BE ENOUGH FOR US TO GET CLEAR AND MEET KISHPAUGH AT THE RENDEZVOUS POINT.
WHAT ARE YOU TALKING ABOUT?
THIS COMES FROM THE TOP -- COMMANDER KISHPAUGH'S ORDERS. HE SAID YOU'D GO ALONG.
ARE YOU GOING TO BE A PROBLEM?
I MIGHT.
WE'RE HERE TO *STOP* A WAR -- NOT START A NEW ONE.

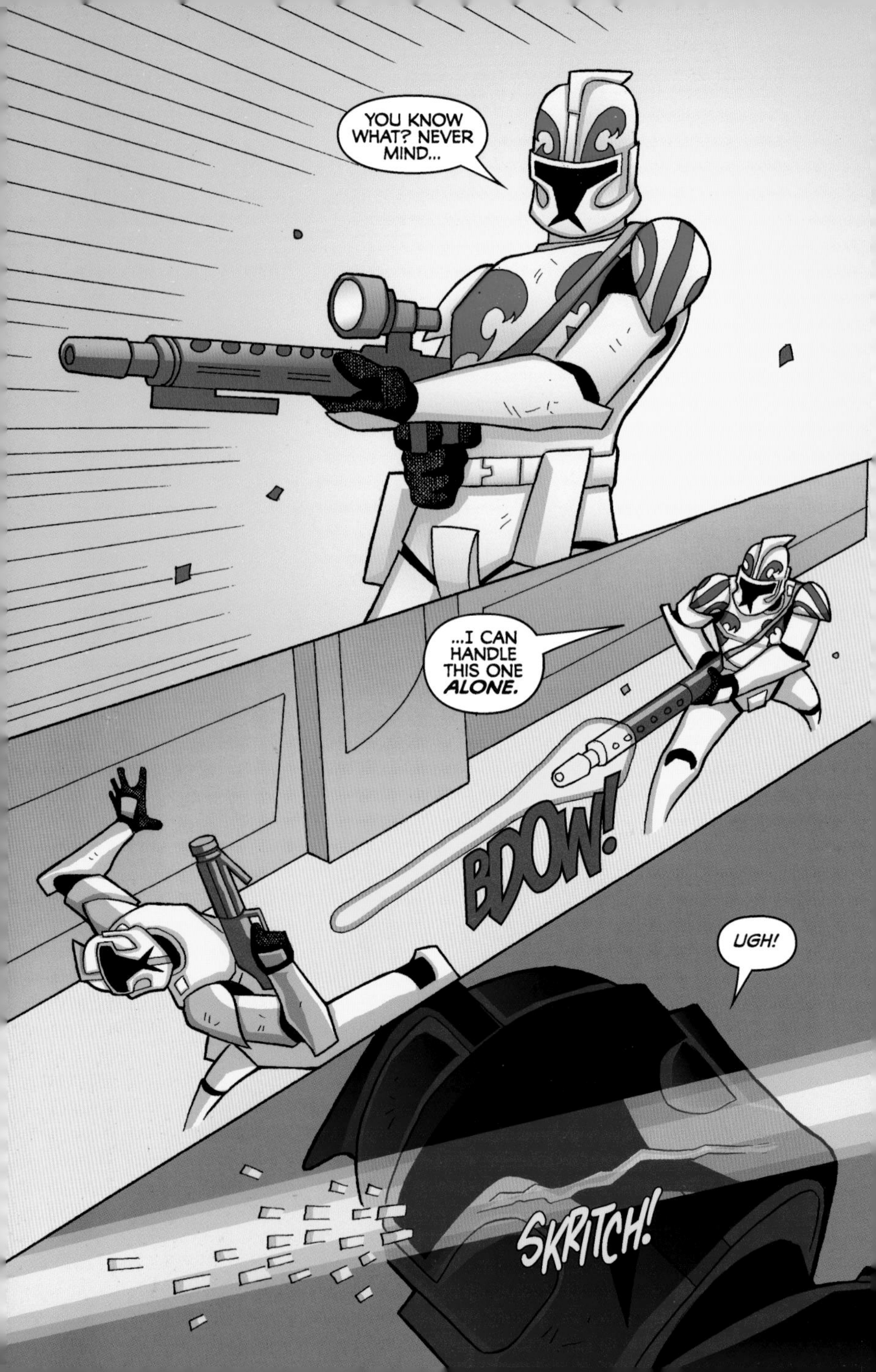
YOU KNOW WHAT? NEVER MIND...
...I CAN HANDLE THIS ONE ALONE.
BDOW!
UGH!
SKRITCH!

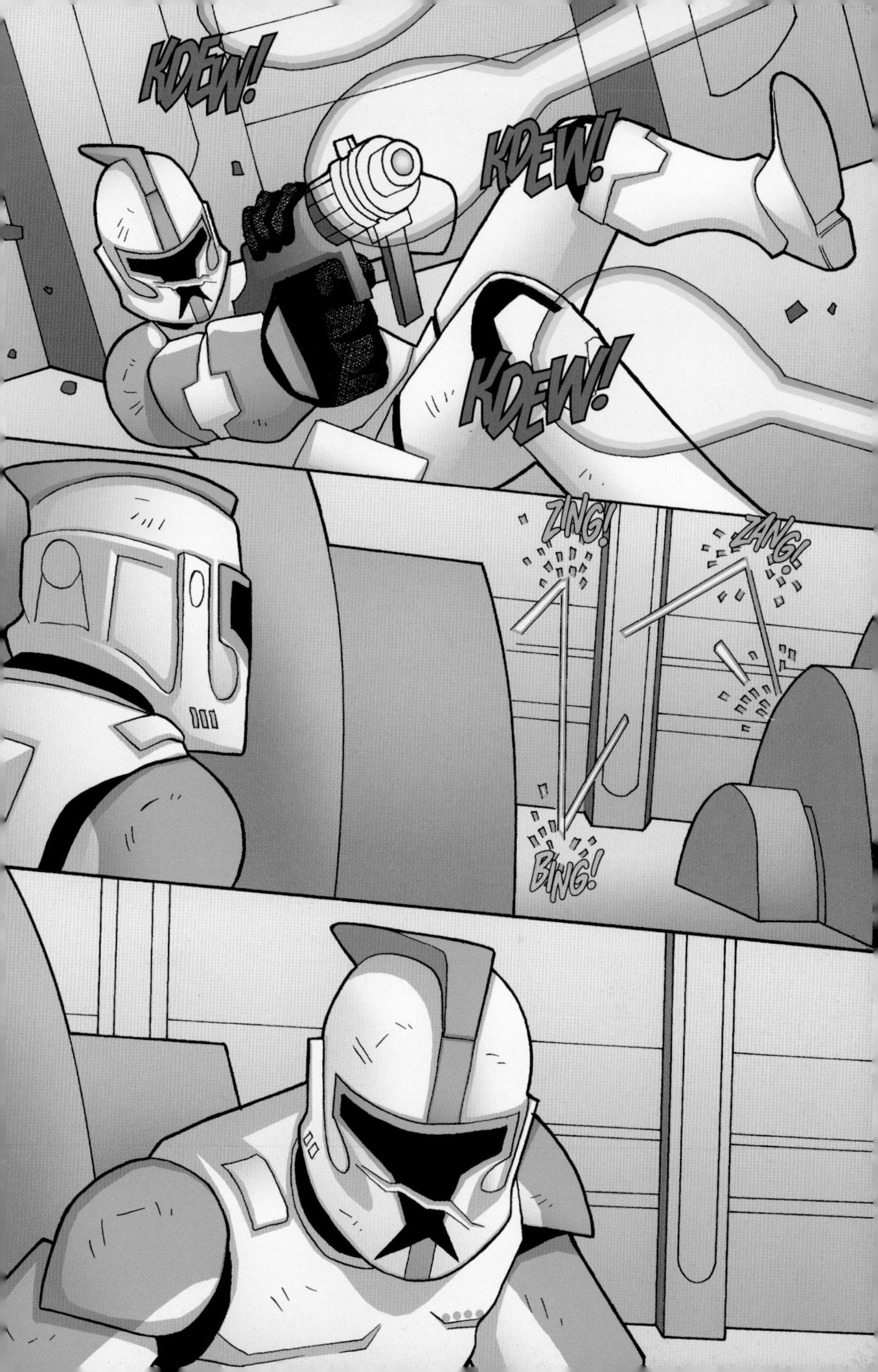

KDEW!
KDEW!
KDEW!
ZING!
ZANG!
BING!

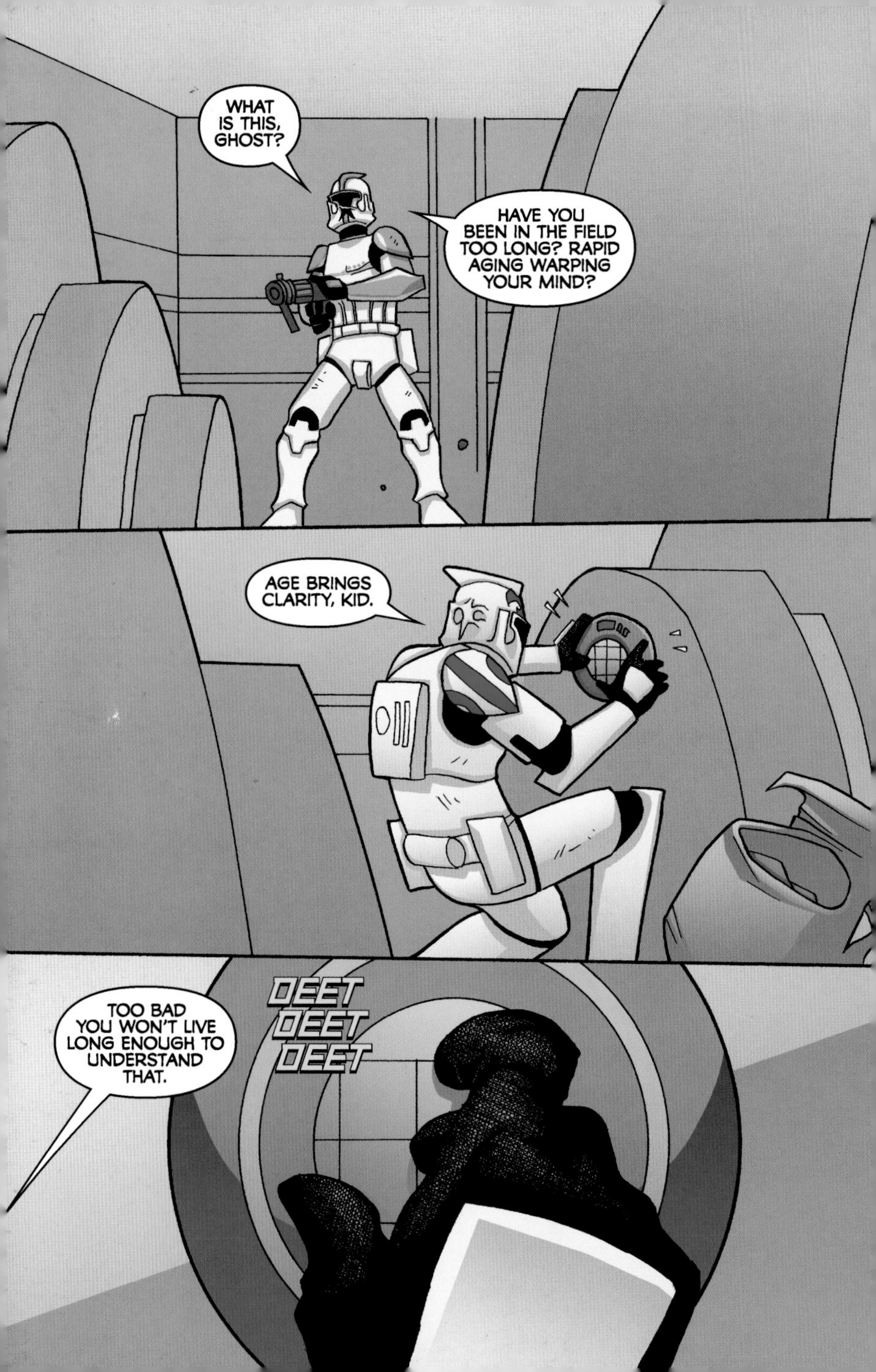
WHAT IS THIS, GHOST?
HAVE YOU BEEN IN THE FIELD TOO LONG? RAPID AGING WARPING YOUR MIND?
AGE BRINGS CLARITY, KID.
TOO BAD YOU WON'T LIVE LONG ENOUGH TO UNDERSTAND THAT.
DEET DEET DEET

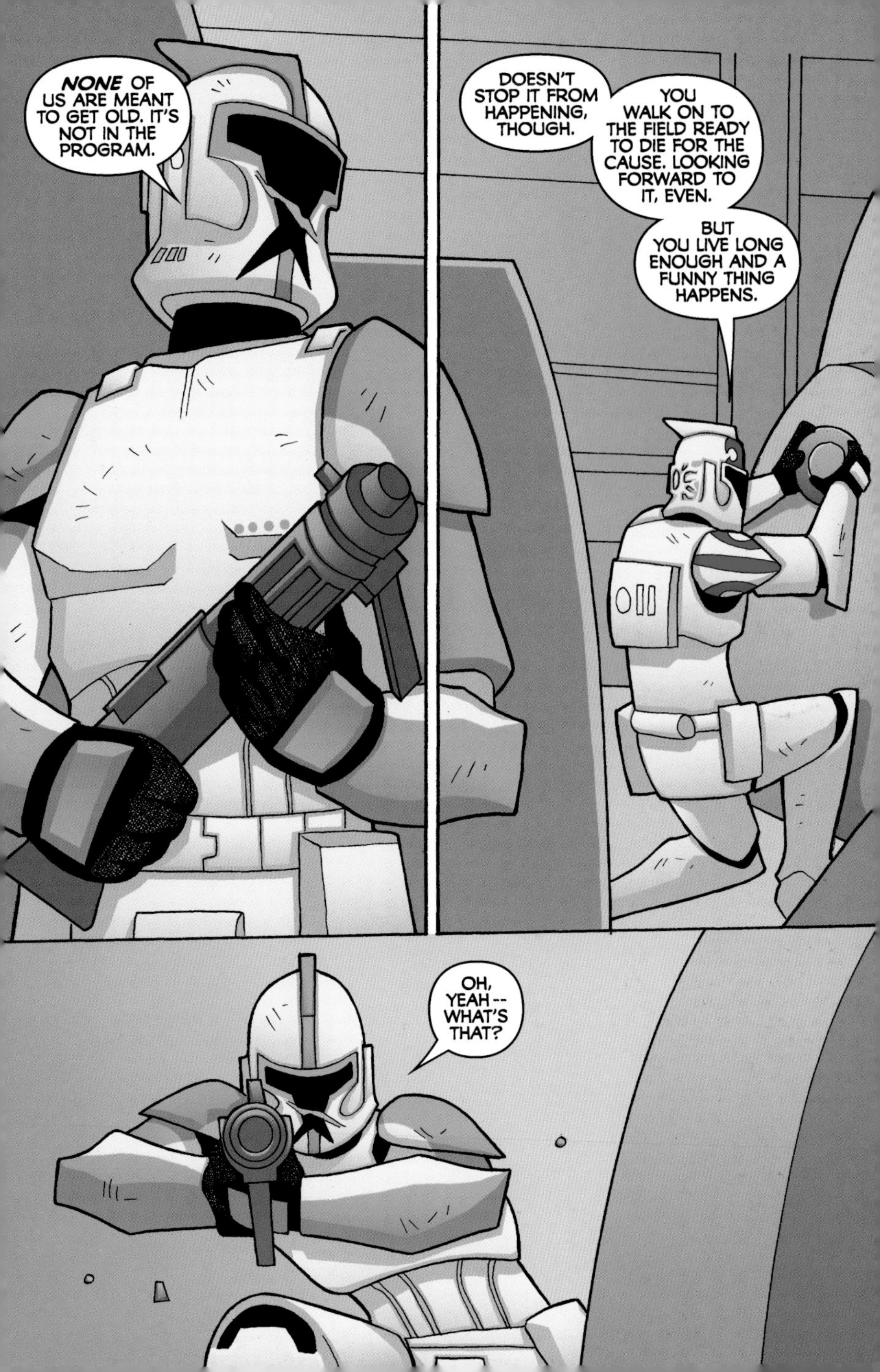
NONE OF US ARE MEANT TO GET OLD. IT'S NOT IN THE PROGRAM.
DOESN'T STOP IT FROM HAPPENING, THOUGH.
YOU WALK ON TO THE FIELD READY TO DIE FOR THE CAUSE. LOOKING FORWARD TO IT, EVEN.
BUT YOU LIVE LONG ENOUGH AND A FUNNY THING HAPPENS.
OH, YEAH -- WHAT'S THAT?

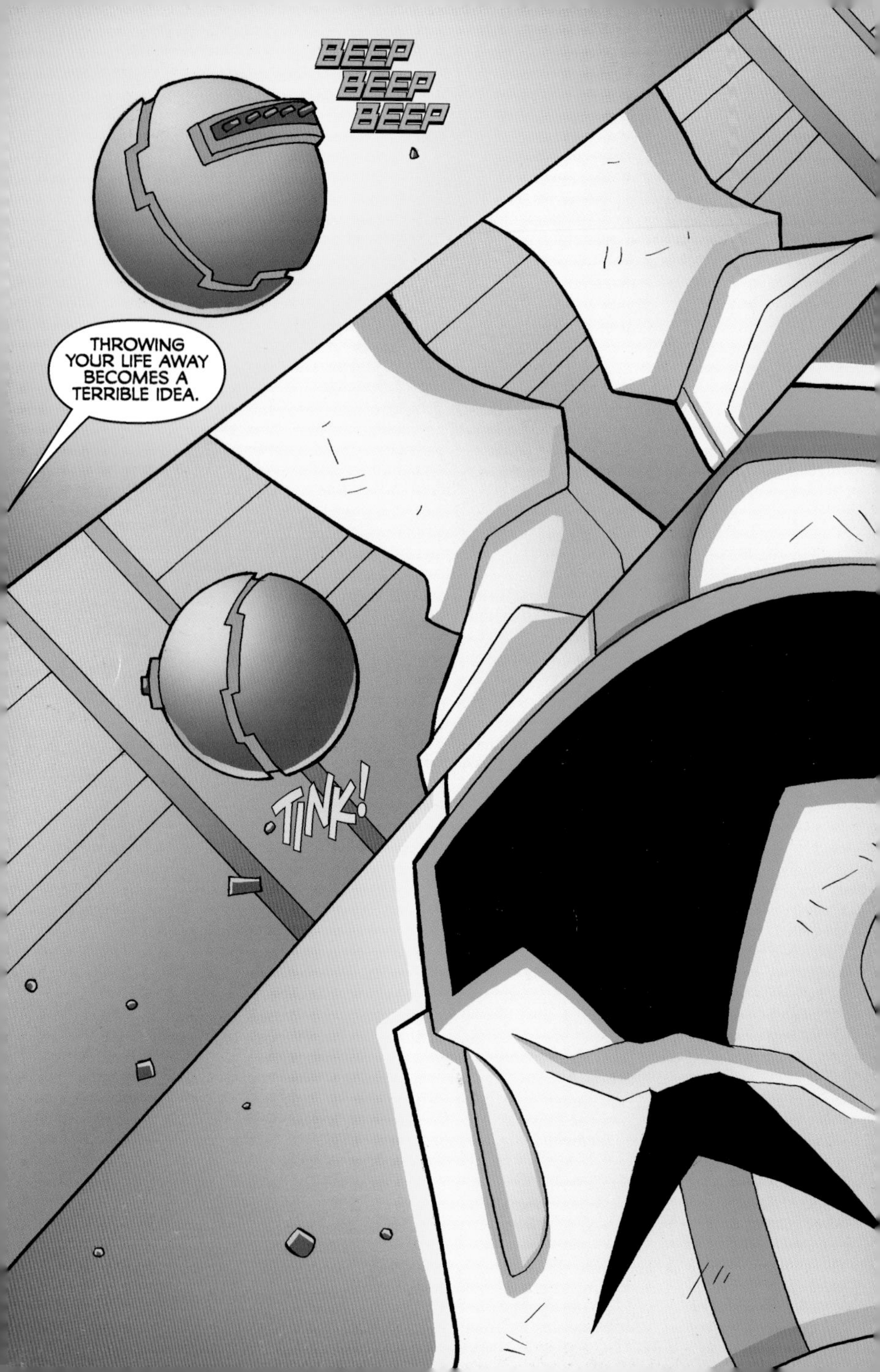
BEEP
BEEP
BEEP
THROWING YOUR LIFE AWAY BECOMES A TERRIBLE IDEA.
TINK!

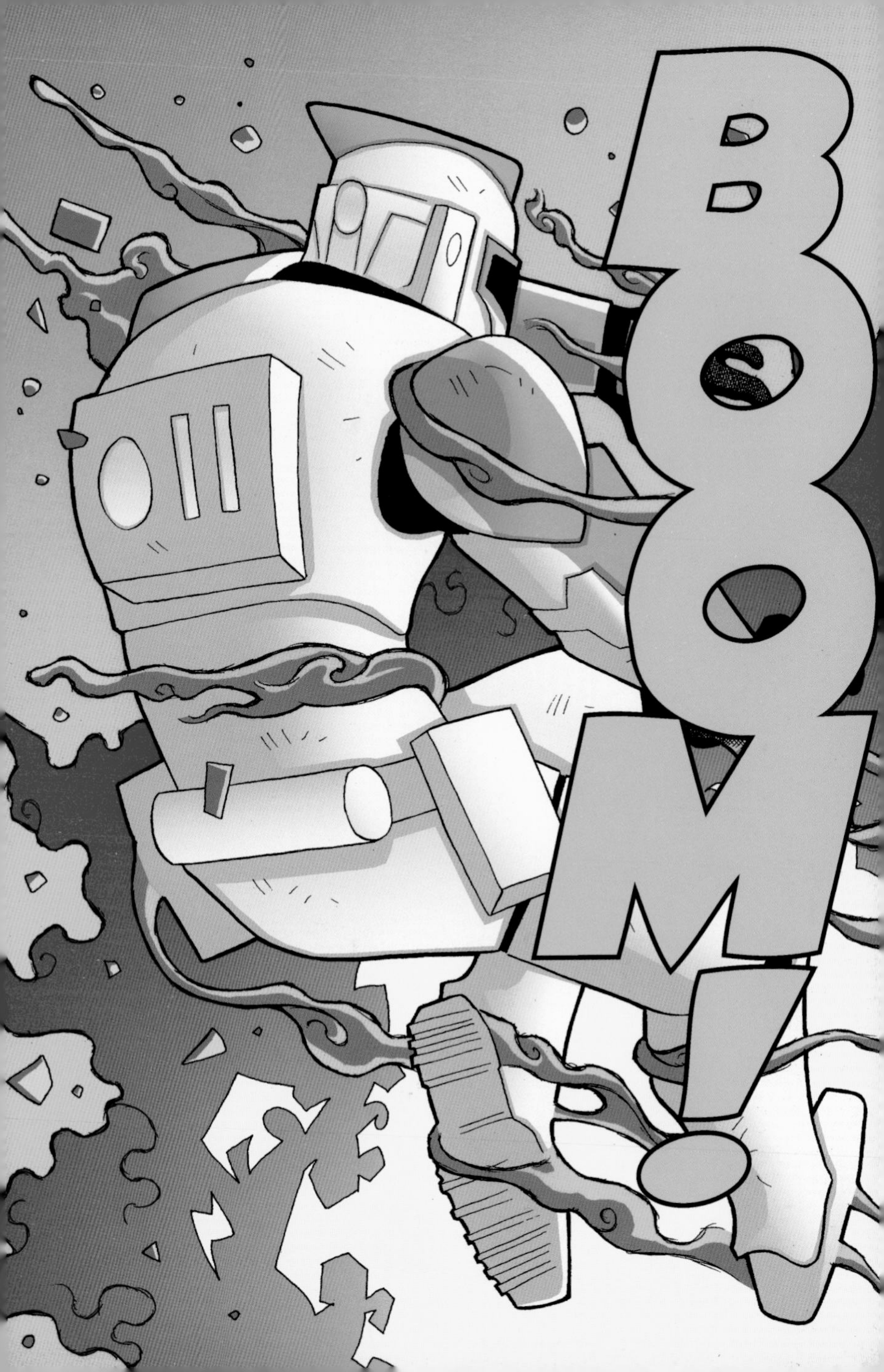
BOOM!

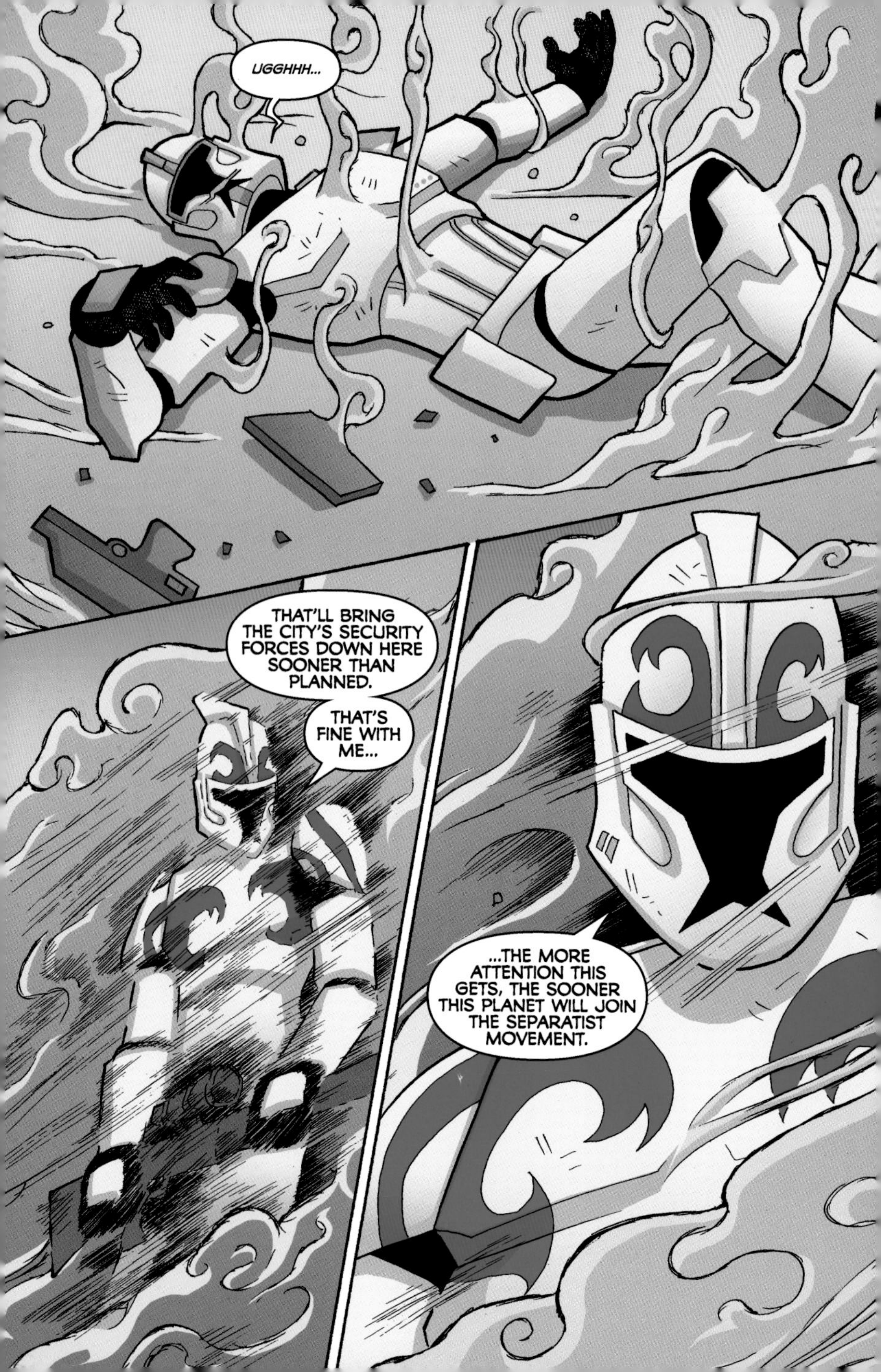
UGGHHH...
THAT'LL BRING THE CITY'S SECURITY FORCES DOWN HERE SOONER THAN PLANNED.
THAT'S FINE WITH ME...
...THE MORE ATTENTION THIS GETS, THE SOONER THIS PLANET WILL JOIN THE SEPARATIST MOVEMENT.

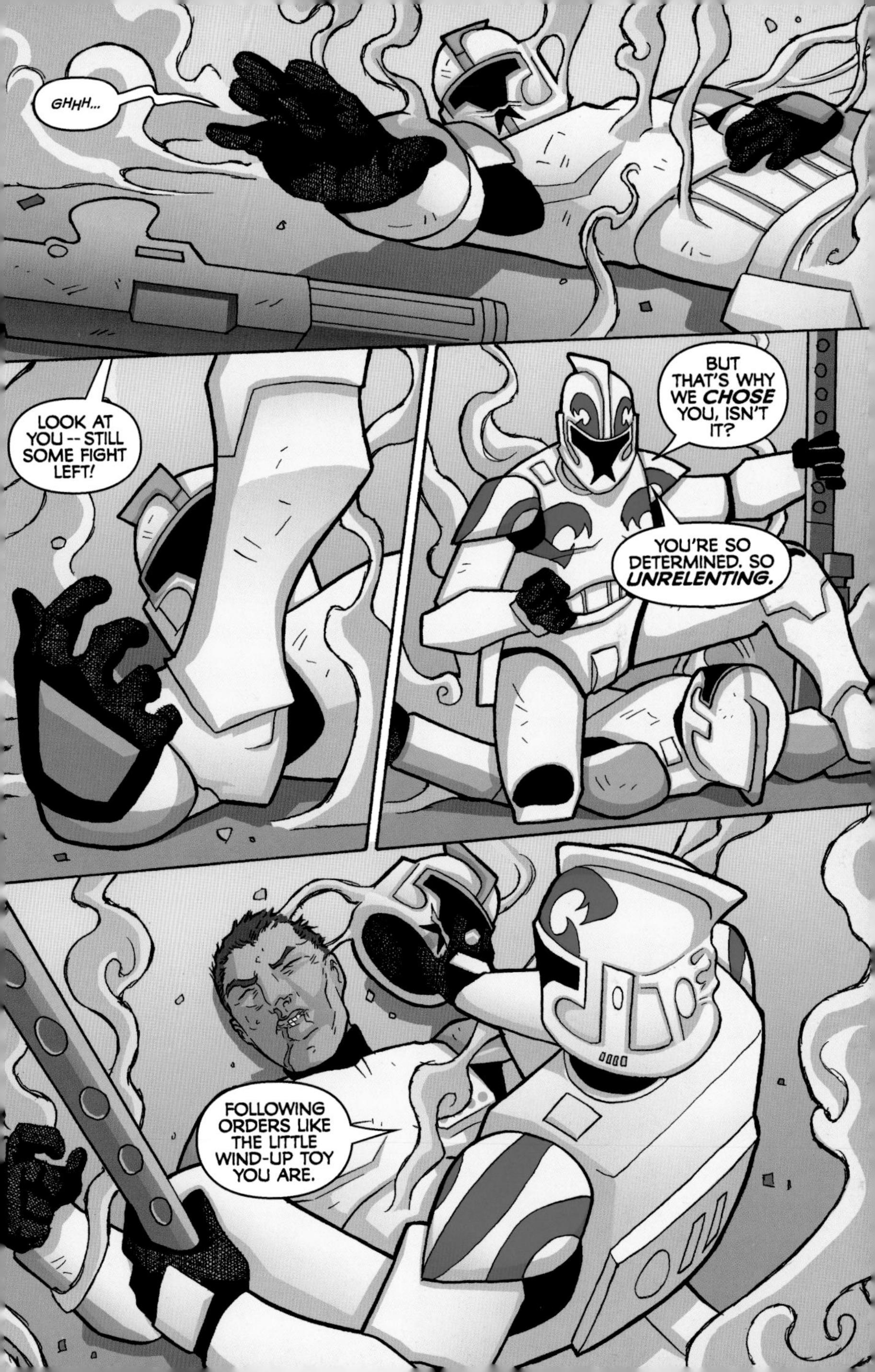

GHHH...
LOOK AT YOU -- STILL SOME FIGHT LEFT!
BUT THAT'S WHY WE *CHOSE* YOU, ISN'T IT?
YOU'RE SO DETERMINED. SO *UNRELENTING.*
FOLLOWING ORDERS LIKE THE LITTLE WIND-UP TOY YOU ARE.

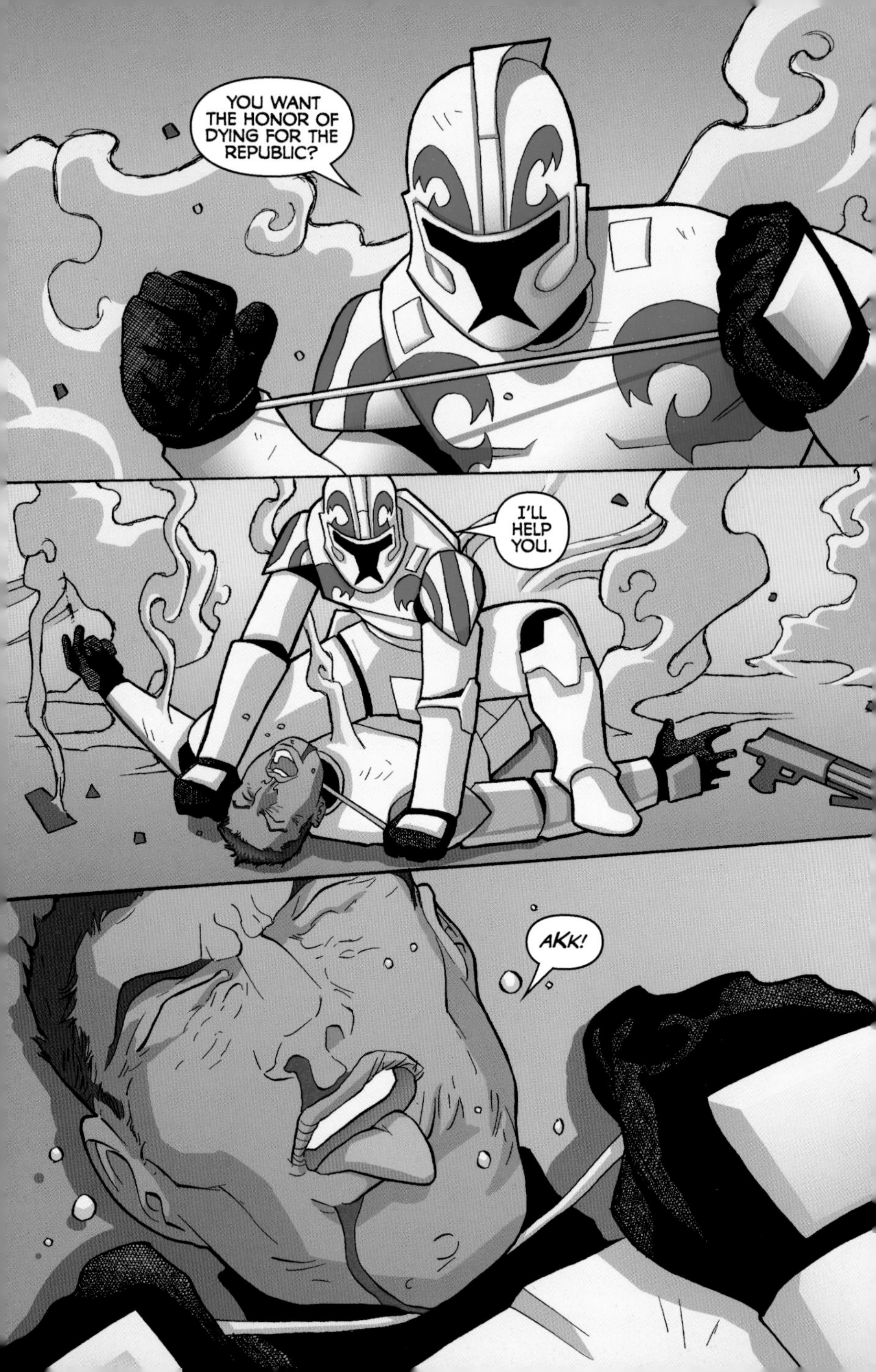
YOU WANT THE HONOR OF DYING FOR THE REPUBLIC?
I'LL HELP YOU.
AKK!

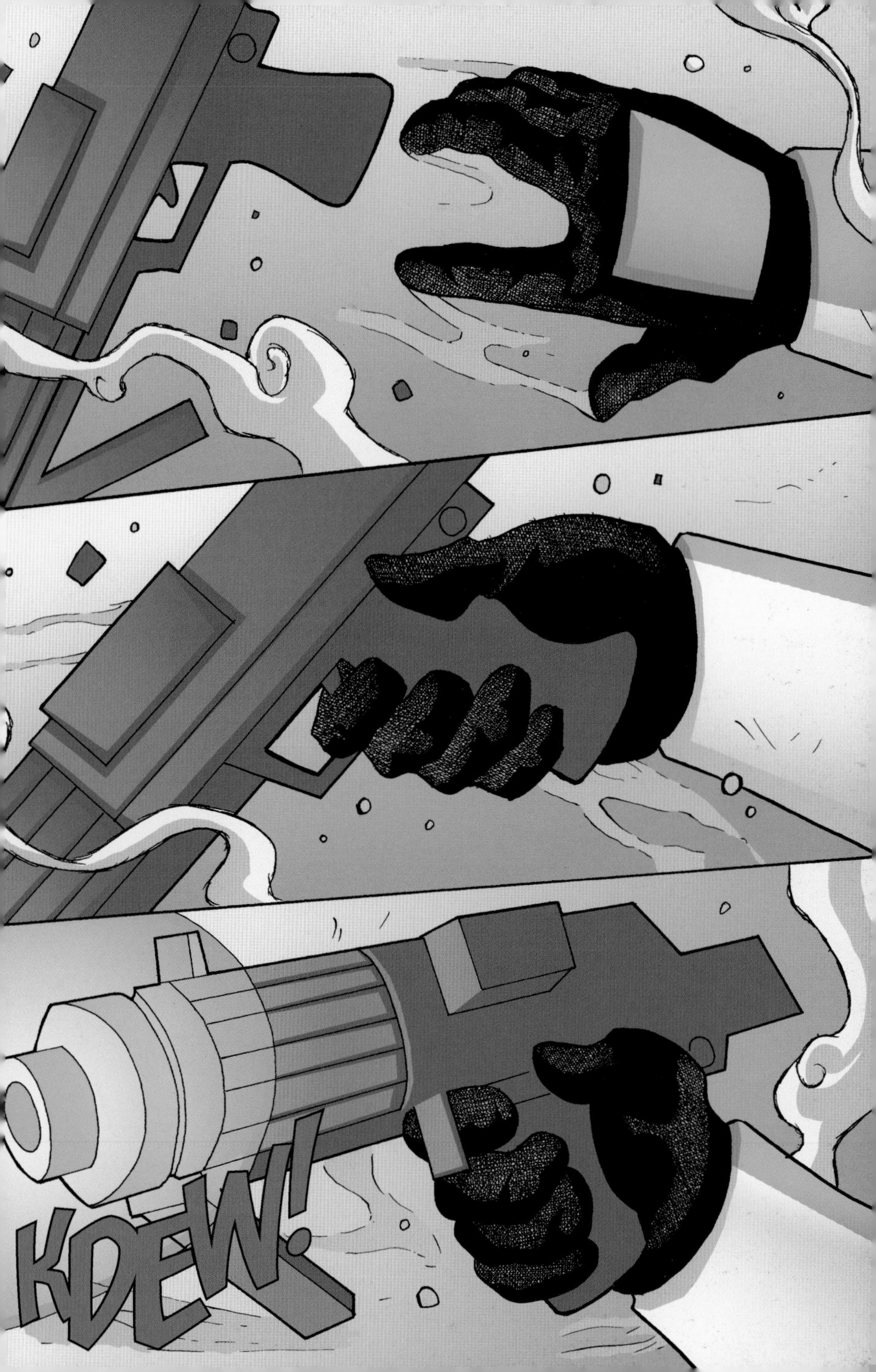
KDEW!

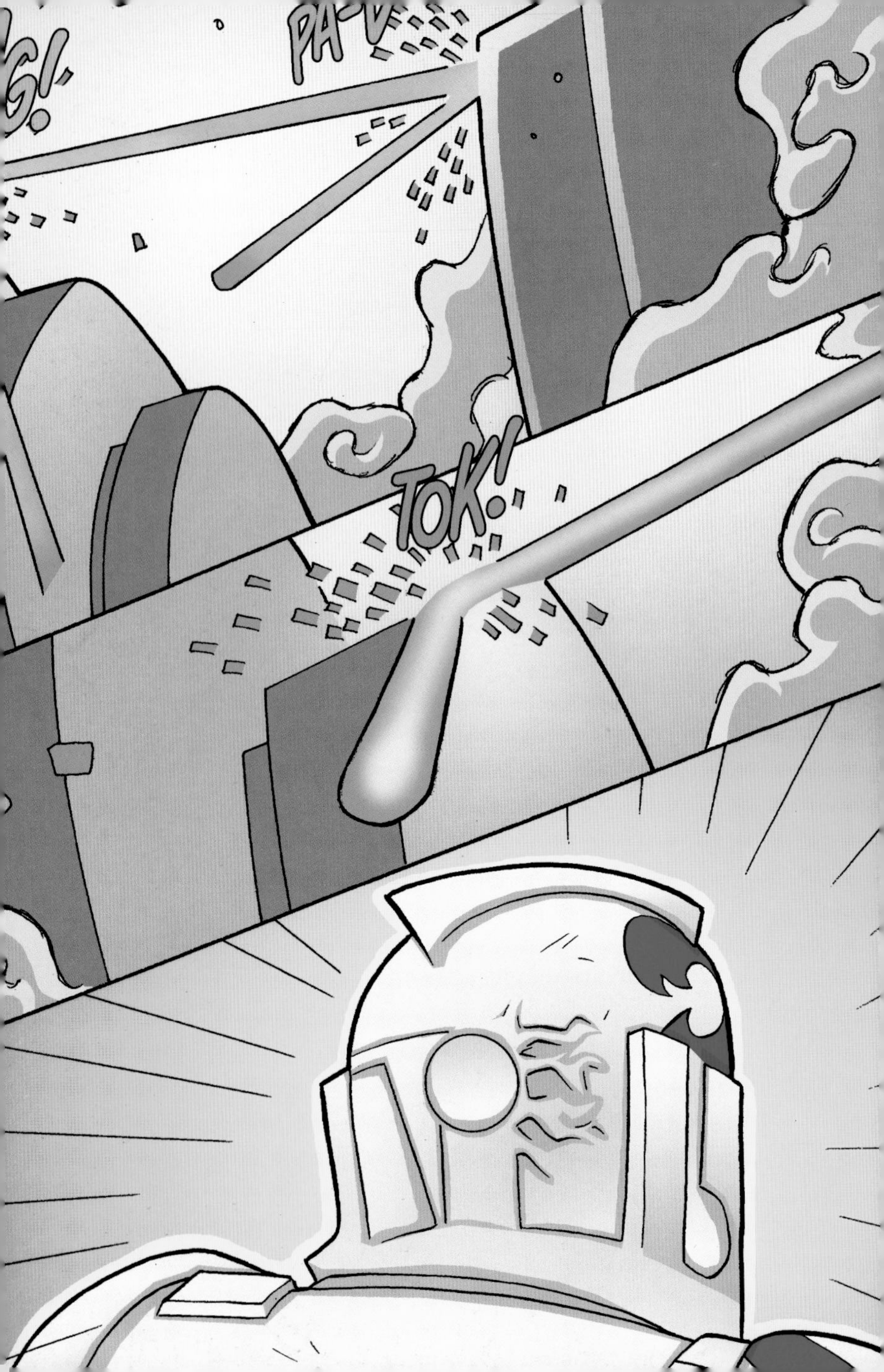
G!
PA-
TOK!

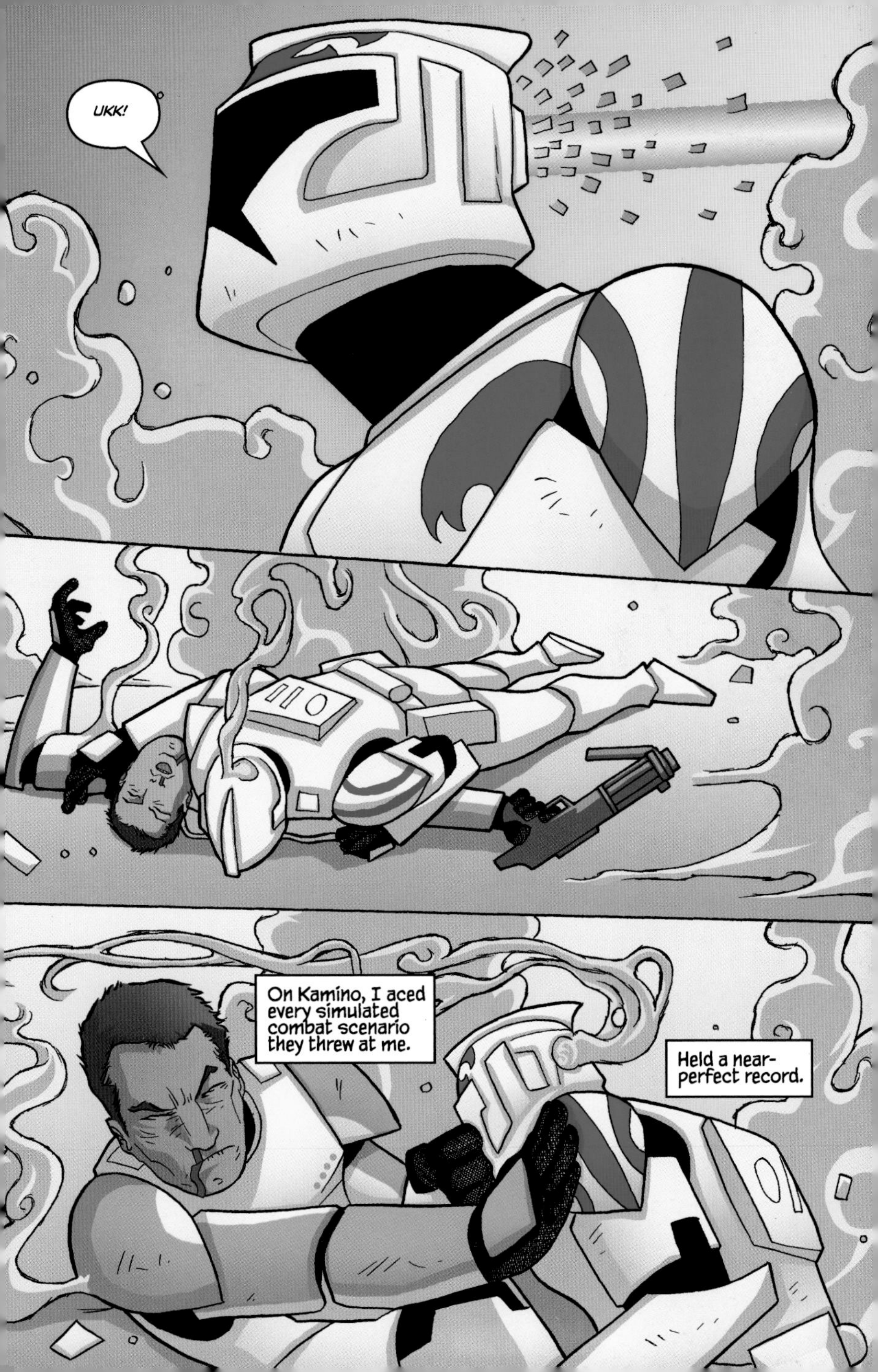
UKK!
On Kamino, I aced every simulated combat scenario they threw at me.
Held a near-perfect record.

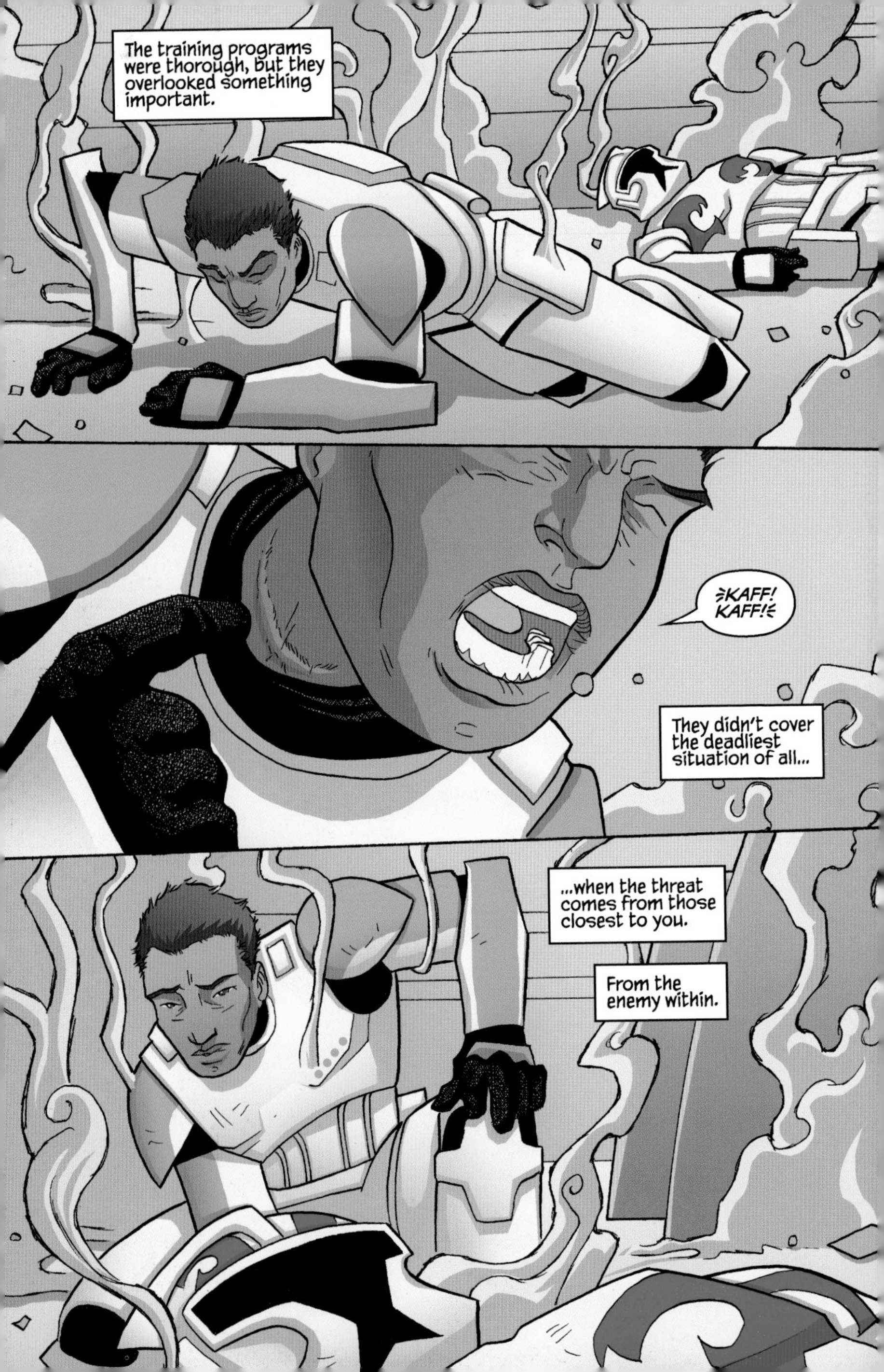
The training programs were thorough, but they overlooked something important.
KAFF! KAFF!
They didn't cover the deadliest situation of all...
...when the threat comes from those closest to you.
From the enemy within.

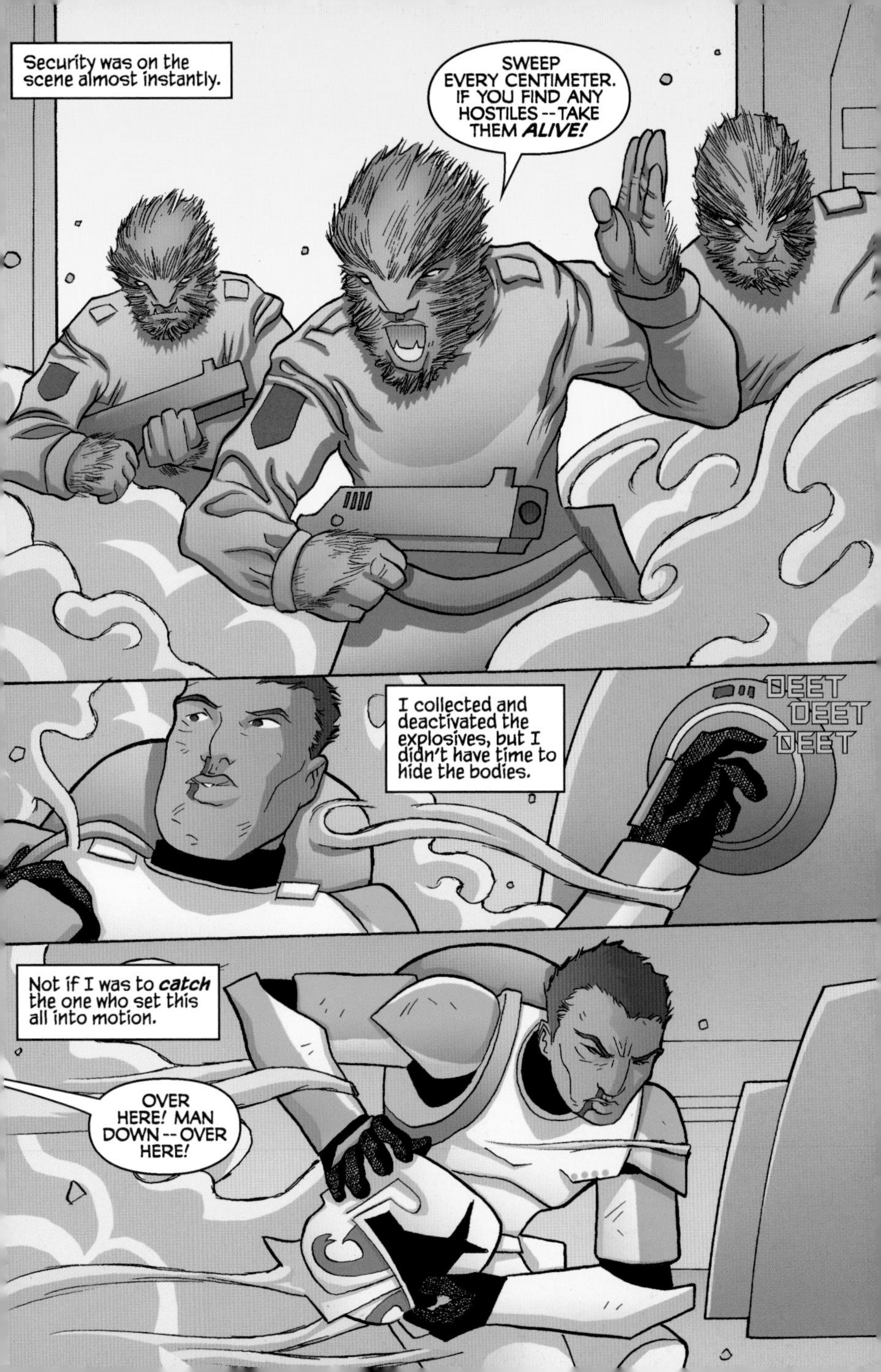
Security was on the scene almost instantly.
SWEEP EVERY CENTIMETER. IF YOU FIND ANY HOSTILES -- TAKE THEM *ALIVE!*
I collected and deactivated the explosives, but I didn't have time to hide the bodies.
DEET DEET DEET
Not if I was to *catch* the one who set this all into motion.
OVER HERE! MAN DOWN -- OVER HERE!

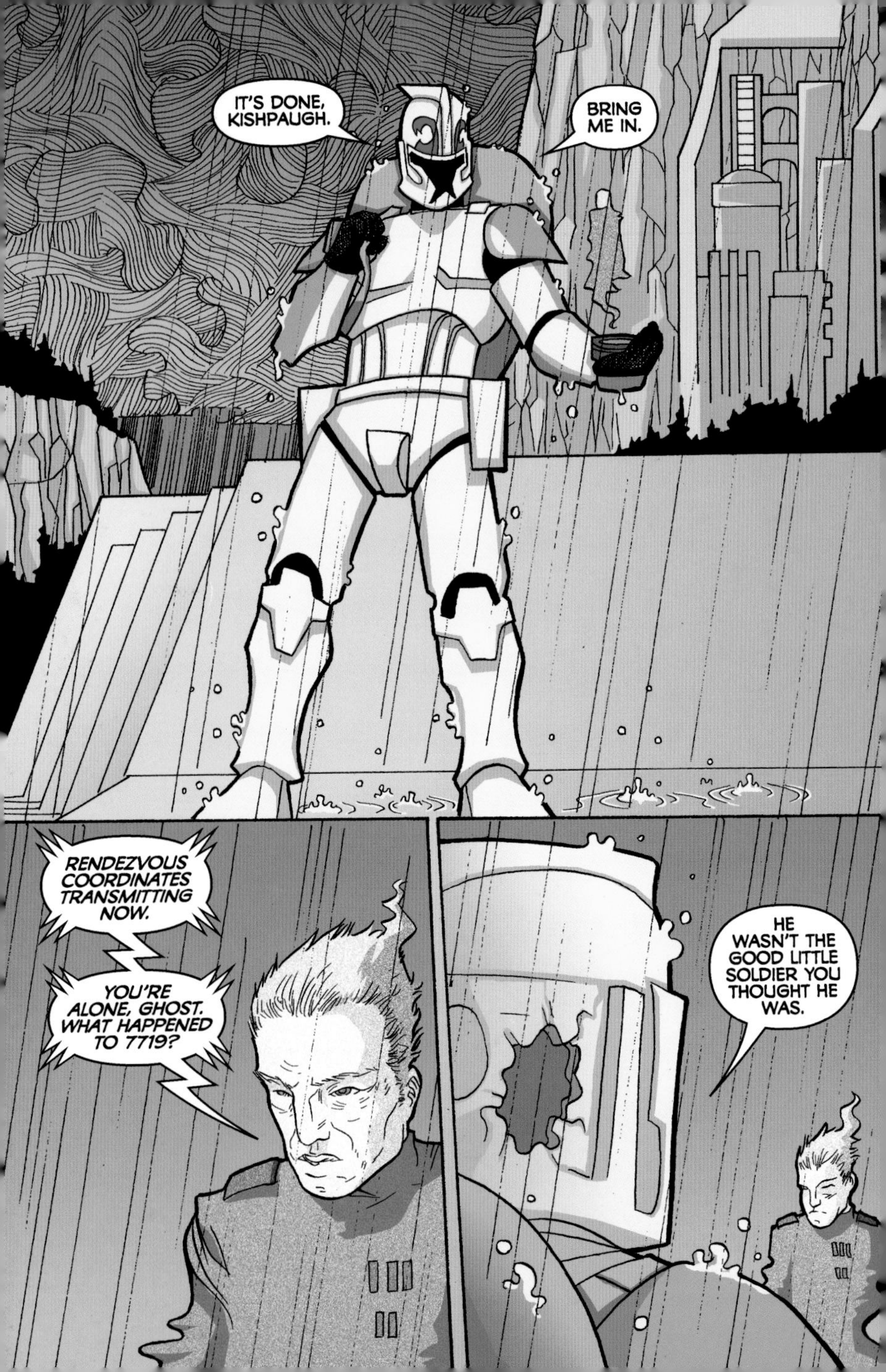
IT'S DONE, KISHPAUGH.
BRING ME IN.
RENDEZVOUS COORDINATES TRANSMITTING NOW.
YOU'RE ALONE, GHOST. WHAT HAPPENED TO 7719?
HE WASN'T THE GOOD LITTLE SOLDIER YOU THOUGHT HE WAS.

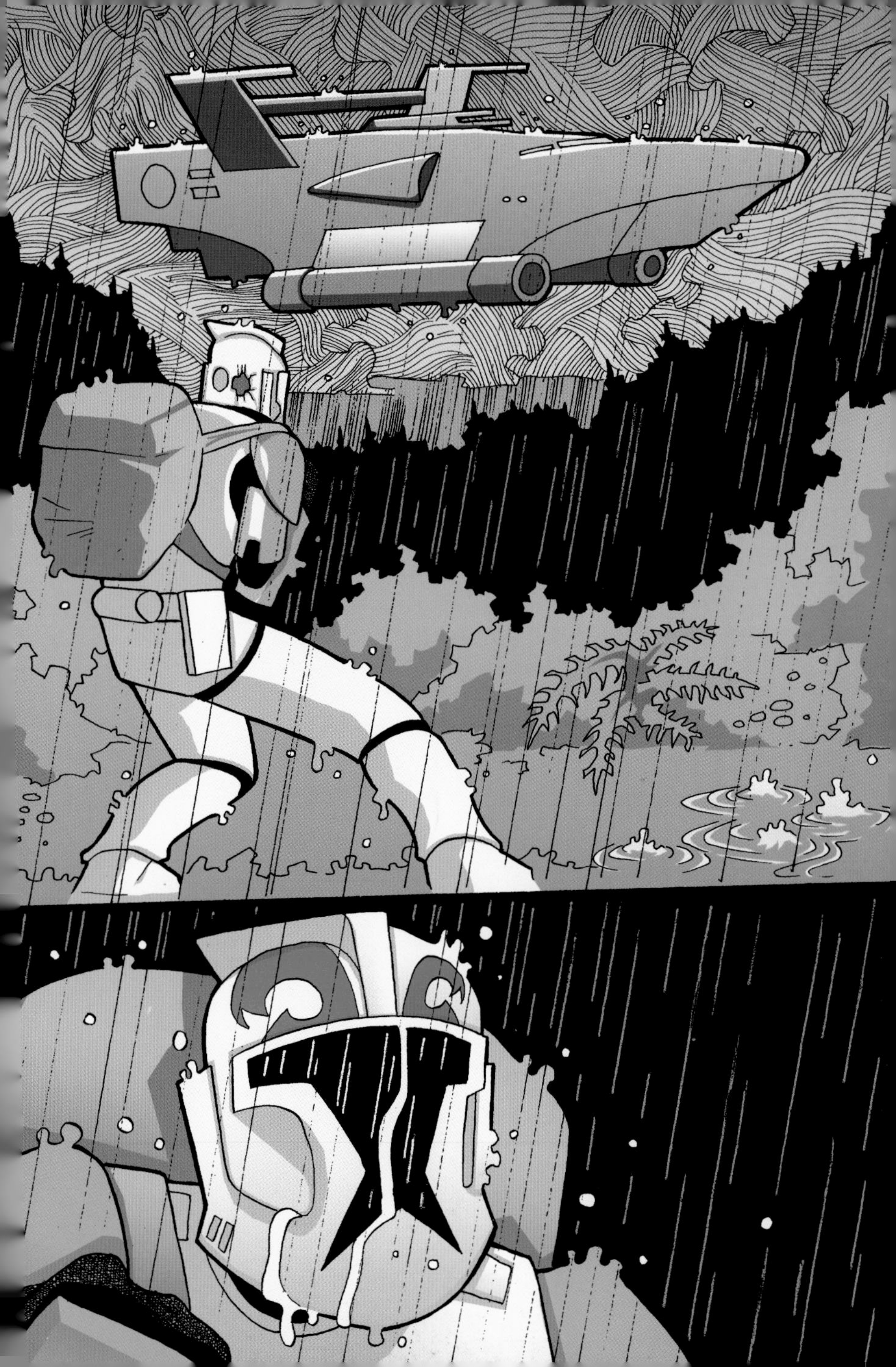

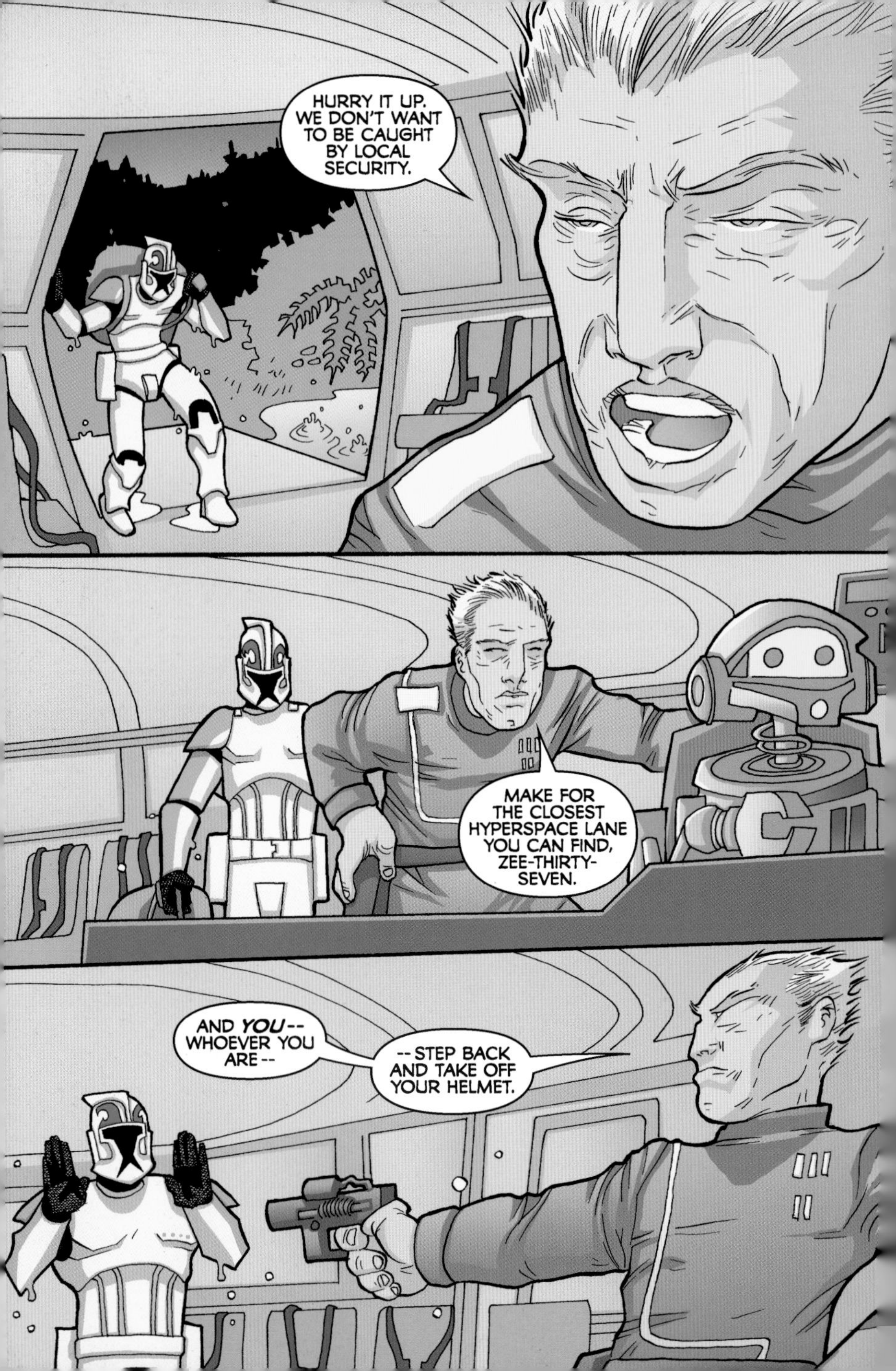
HURRY IT UP. WE DON'T WANT TO BE CAUGHT BY LOCAL SECURITY.
MAKE FOR THE CLOSEST HYPERSPACE LANE YOU CAN FIND, ZEE-THIRTY-SEVEN.
AND *YOU*-- WHOEVER YOU ARE--
--STEP BACK AND TAKE OFF YOUR HELMET.

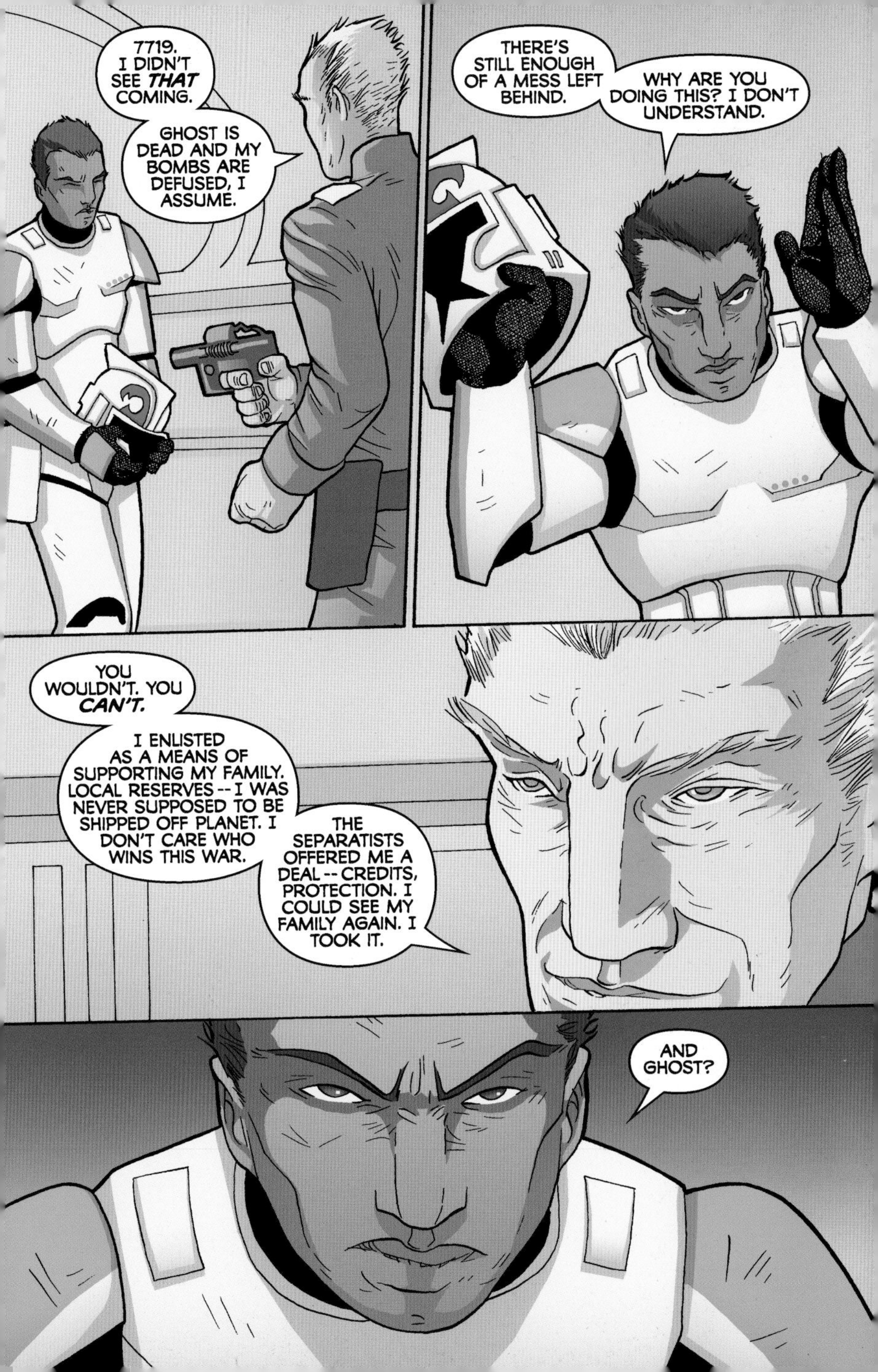
7719. I DIDN'T SEE *THAT* COMING.
GHOST IS DEAD AND MY BOMBS ARE DEFUSED, I ASSUME.
THERE'S STILL ENOUGH OF A MESS LEFT BEHIND.
WHY ARE YOU DOING THIS? I DON'T UNDERSTAND.
YOU WOULDN'T. YOU *CAN'T.*
I ENLISTED AS A MEANS OF SUPPORTING MY FAMILY. LOCAL RESERVES -- I WAS NEVER SUPPOSED TO BE SHIPPED OFF PLANET. I DON'T CARE WHO WINS THIS WAR.
THE SEPARATISTS OFFERED ME A DEAL -- CREDITS, PROTECTION. I COULD SEE MY FAMILY AGAIN. I TOOK IT.
AND GHOST?

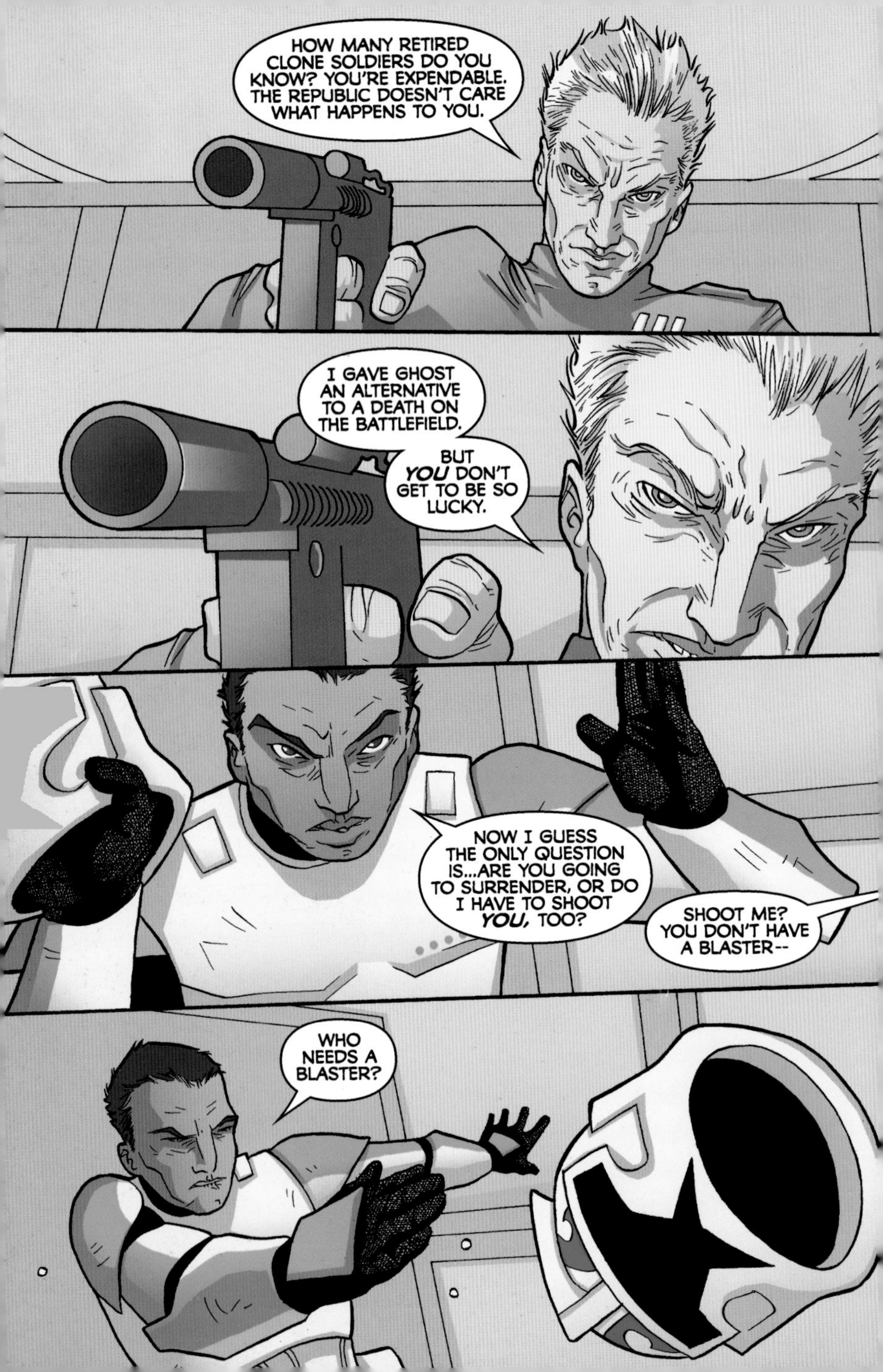
HOW MANY RETIRED CLONE SOLDIERS DO YOU KNOW? YOU'RE EXPENDABLE. THE REPUBLIC DOESN'T CARE WHAT HAPPENS TO YOU.
I GAVE GHOST AN ALTERNATIVE TO A DEATH ON THE BATTLEFIELD.
BUT *YOU* DON'T GET TO BE SO LUCKY.
NOW I GUESS THE ONLY QUESTION IS...ARE YOU GOING TO SURRENDER, OR DO I HAVE TO SHOOT *YOU,* TOO?
SHOOT ME? YOU DON'T HAVE A BLASTER--
WHO NEEDS A BLASTER?

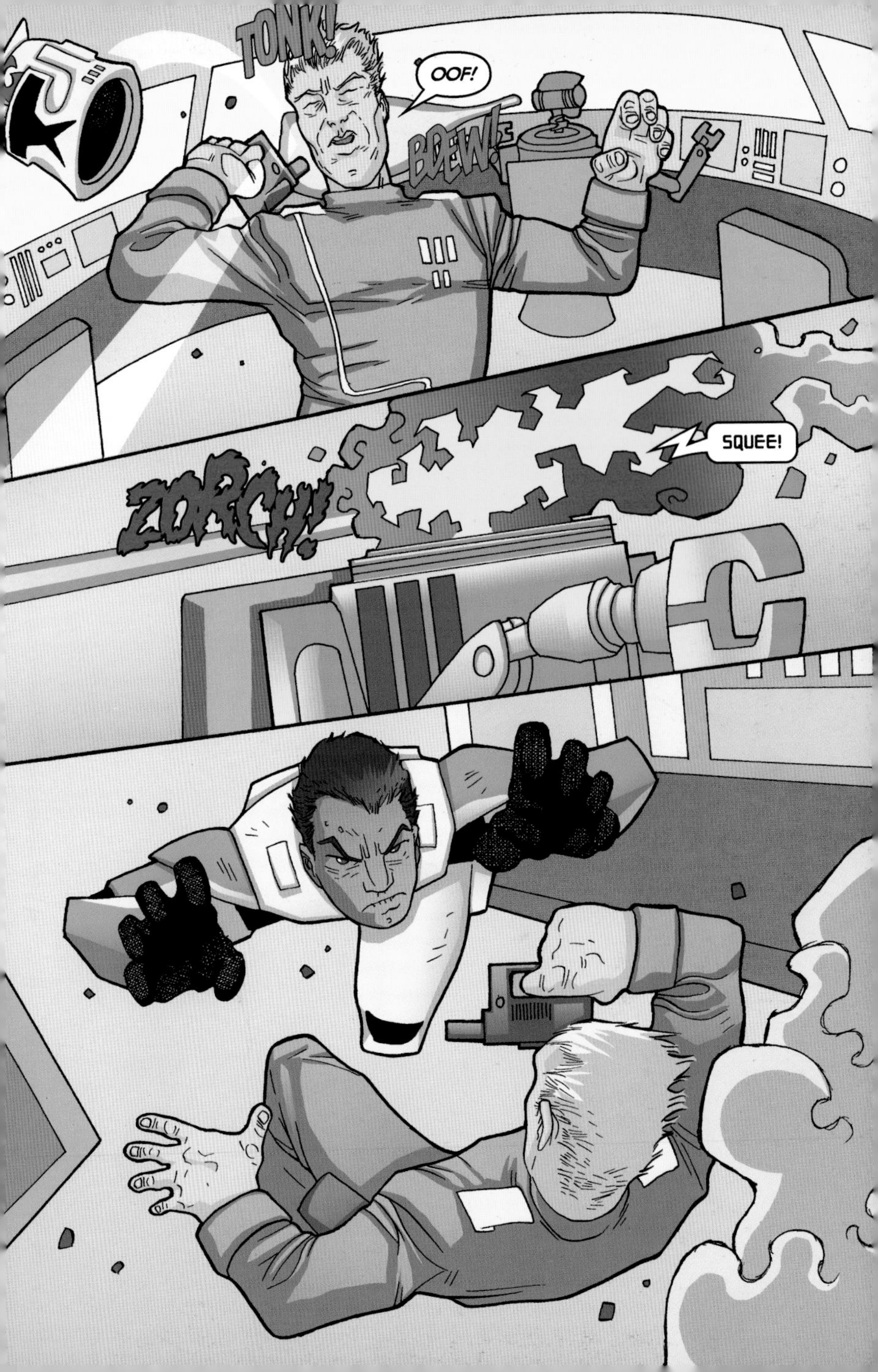
TONK!
OOF!
BDEW!
ZORCH!
SQUEE!

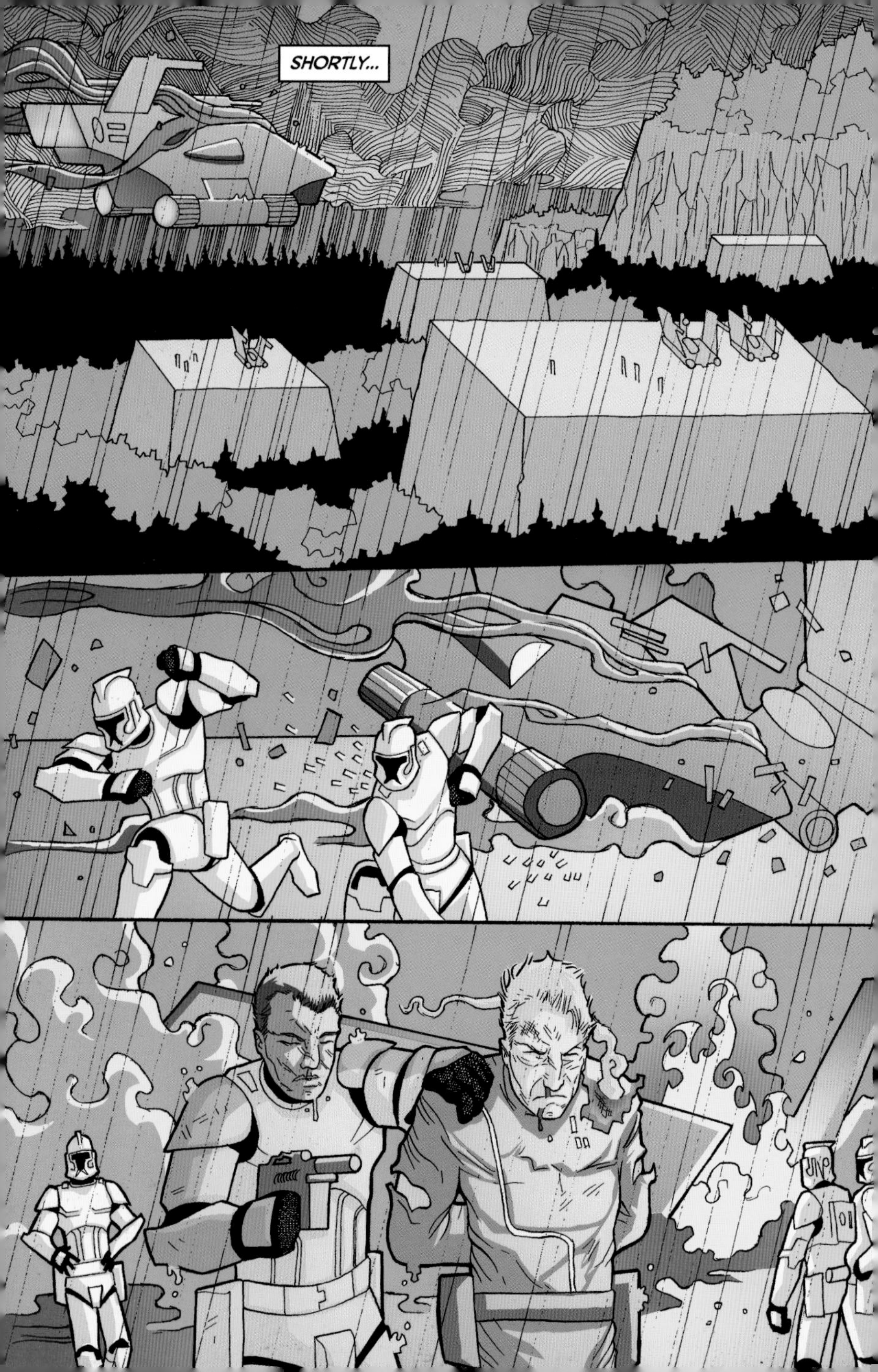
SHORTLY...

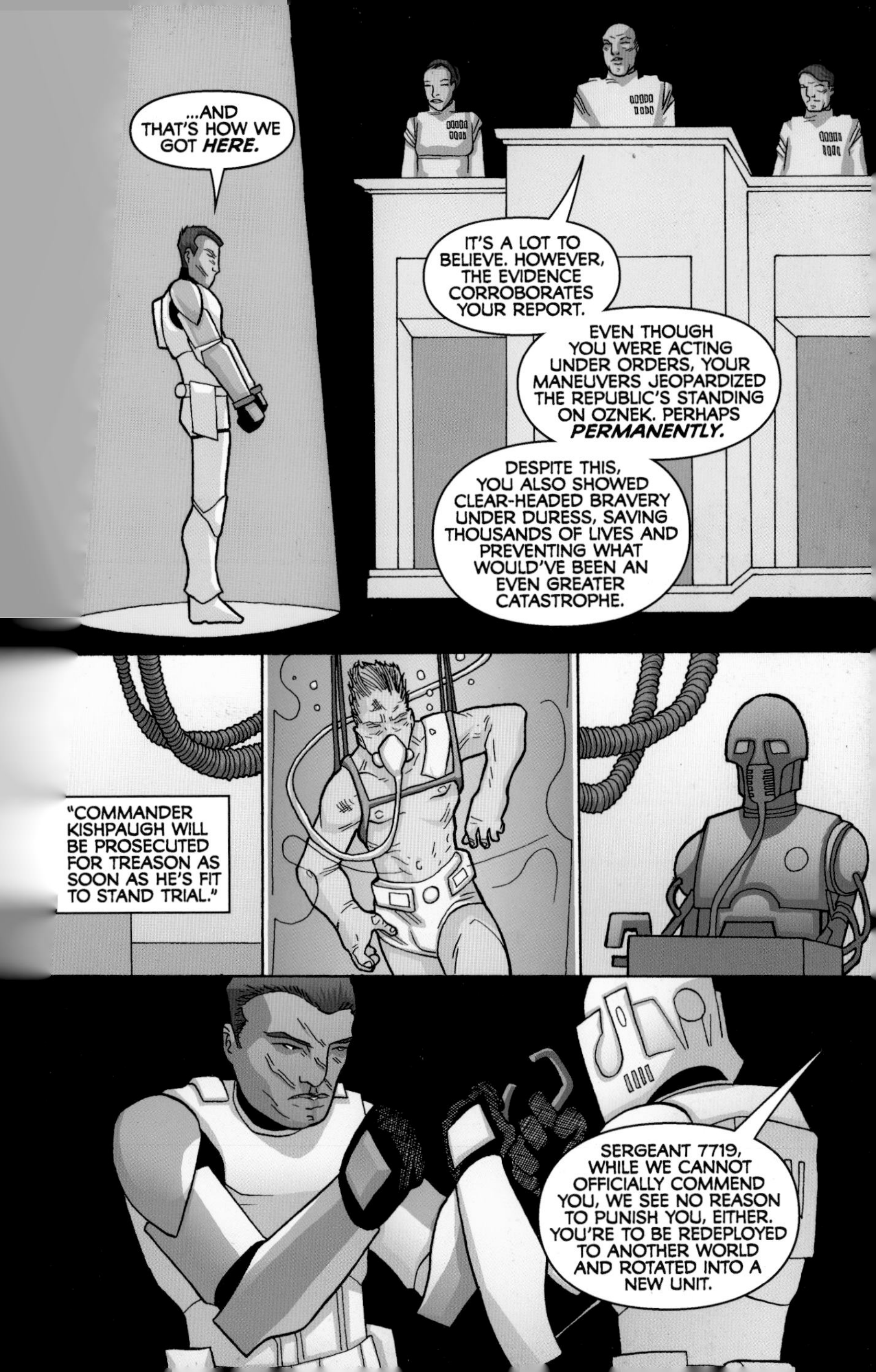
...AND THAT'S HOW WE GOT *HERE.*
IT'S A LOT TO BELIEVE. HOWEVER, THE EVIDENCE CORROBORATES YOUR REPORT.
EVEN THOUGH YOU WERE ACTING UNDER ORDERS, YOUR MANEUVERS JEOPARDIZED THE REPUBLIC'S STANDING ON OZNEK. PERHAPS *PERMANENTLY.*
DESPITE THIS, YOU ALSO SHOWED CLEAR-HEADED BRAVERY UNDER DURESS, SAVING THOUSANDS OF LIVES AND PREVENTING WHAT WOULD'VE BEEN AN EVEN GREATER CATASTROPHE.
"COMMANDER KISHPAUGH WILL BE PROSECUTED FOR TREASON AS SOON AS HE'S FIT TO STAND TRIAL."
SERGEANT 7719, WHILE WE CANNOT OFFICIALLY COMMEND YOU, WE SEE NO REASON TO PUNISH YOU, EITHER. YOU'RE TO BE REDEPLOYED TO ANOTHER WORLD AND ROTATED INTO A NEW UNIT.

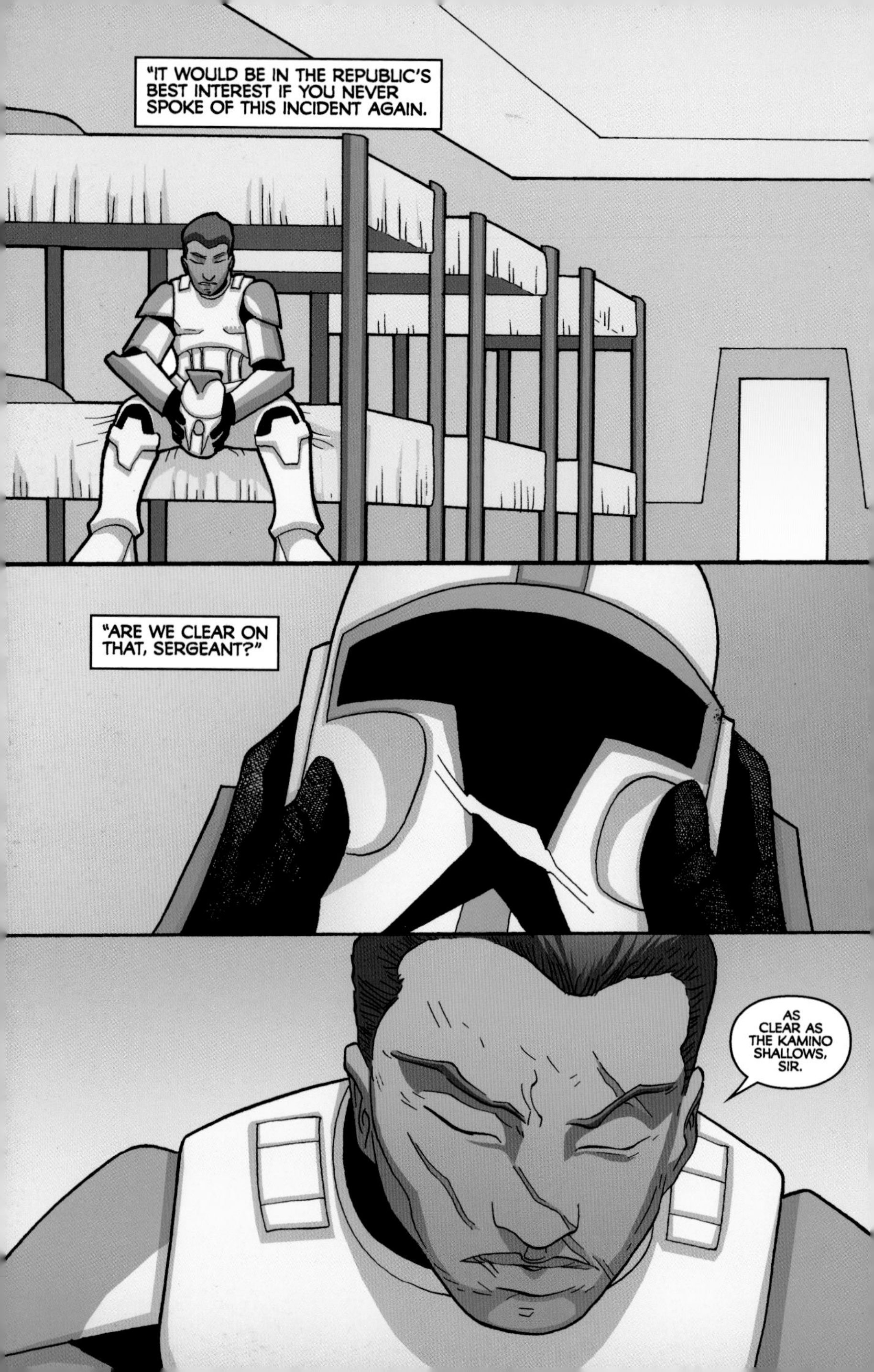
"IT WOULD BE IN THE REPUBLIC'S BEST INTEREST IF YOU NEVER SPOKE OF THIS INCIDENT AGAIN.
"ARE WE CLEAR ON THAT, SERGEANT?"
AS CLEAR AS THE KAMINO SHALLOWS, SIR.

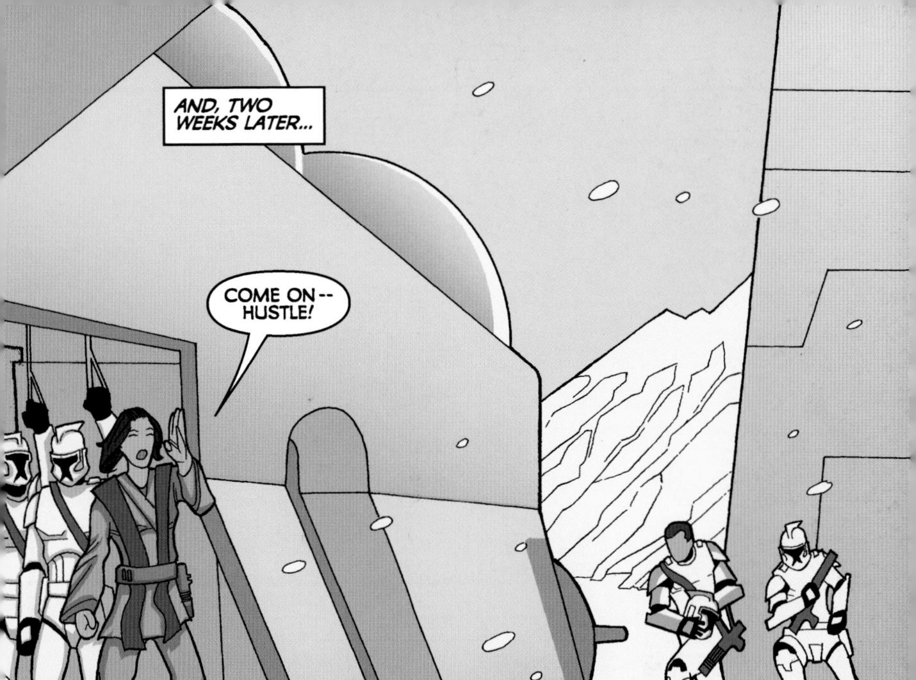
AND, TWO WEEKS LATER...
COME ON -- HUSTLE!

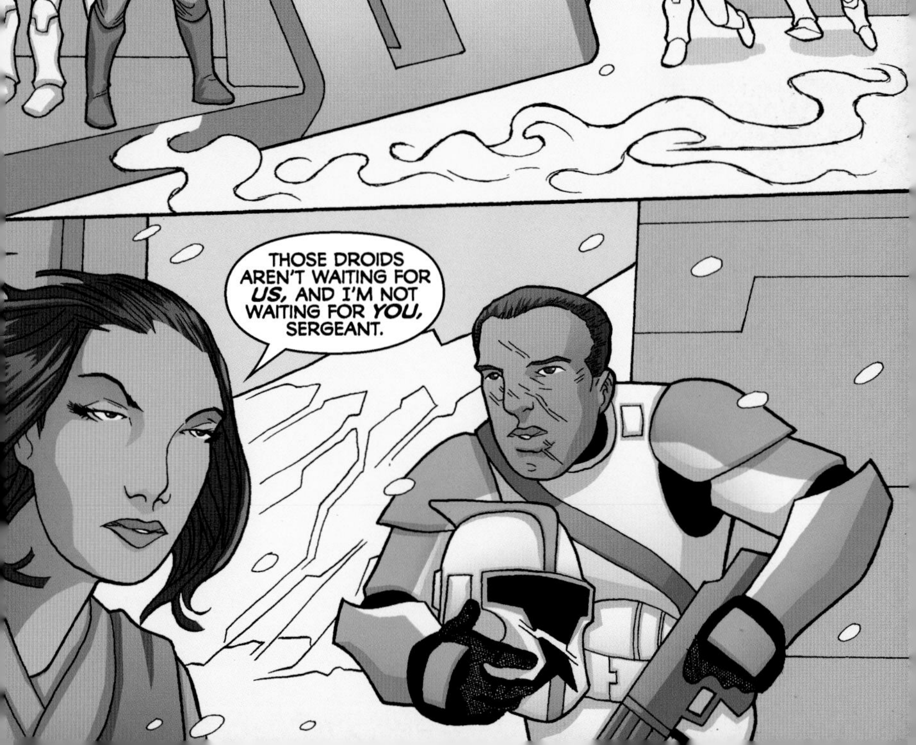
THOSE DROIDS AREN'T WAITING FOR *US,* AND I'M NOT WAITING FOR *YOU,* SERGEANT.

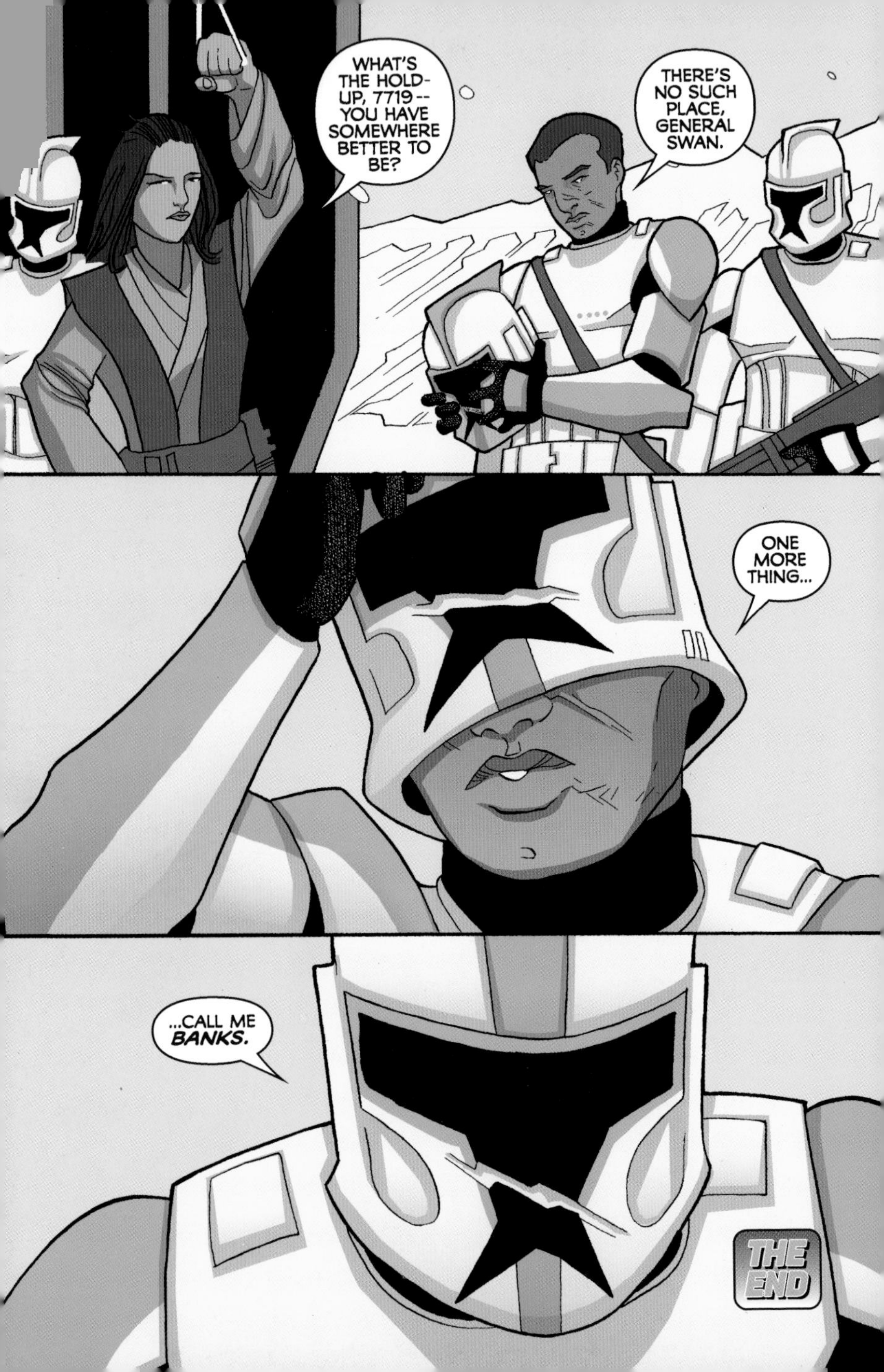
WHAT'S THE HOLD-UP, 7719-- YOU HAVE SOMEWHERE BETTER TO BE?
THERE'S NO SUCH PLACE, GENERAL SWAN.
ONE MORE THING...
...CALL ME *BANKS.*
THE END

STAR WARS GRAPHIC NOVEL TIMELINE (IN YEARS)

Omnibus: Tales of the Jedi—5,000–3,986 BSW4

Knights of the Old Republic—3,964–3,963 BSW4

The Old Republic—3653, 3678 BSW4

Knight Errant—1,032 BSW4

Jedi vs. Sith—1,000 BSW4

Omnibus: Rise of the Sith—33 BSW4

Episode I: The Phantom Menace—32 BSW4

Omnibus: Emissaries and Assassins—32 BSW4

Omnibus: Quinlan Vos—Jedi in Darkness—31–30 BSW4

Omnibus: Menace Revealed—31–22 BSW4

Honor and Duty—22 BSW4

Blood Ties—22 BSW4

Episode II: Attack of the Clones—22 BSW4

Clone Wars—22–19 BSW4

Clone Wars Adventures—22–19 BSW4

General Grievous—22–19 BSW4

Episode III: Revenge of the Sith—19 BSW4

Dark Times—19 BSW4

Omnibus: Droids—5.5 BSW4

Omnibus: Boba Fett—3 BSW4–10 ASW4

Underworld—1 BSW4

Episode IV: A New Hope—SW4

Classic Star Wars—0–3 ASW4

Omnibus: A Long Time Ago . . .—0–4 ASW4

Empire—0 ASW4

Rebellion—0 ASW4

Omnibus: Early Victories—0–3 ASW4

Jabba the Hutt: The Art of the Deal—1 ASW4

Episode V: The Empire Strikes Back—3 ASW4

Omnibus: Shadows of the Empire—3.5–4.5 ASW4

Episode VI: Return of the Jedi—4 ASW4

Omnibus: X-Wing Rogue Squadron—4–5 ASW4

Heir to the Empire—9 ASW4

Dark Force Rising—9 ASW4

The Last Command—9 ASW4

Dark Empire—10 ASW4

Crimson Empire—11 ASW4

Jedi Academy: Leviathan—12 ASW4

Union—19 ASW4

Chewbacca—25 ASW4

Invasion—25 ASW4

Legacy—130–137 ASW4

Old Republic Era
25,000 – 1000 years before
Star Wars: A New Hope

Rise of the Empire Era
1000 – 0 years before
Star Wars: A New Hope

Rebellion Era
0 – 5 years after
Star Wars: A New Hope

New Republic Era
5 – 25 years after
Star Wars: A New Hope

New Jedi Order Era
25+ years after
Star Wars: A New Hope

Legacy Era
130+ years after
Star Wars: A New Hope

Vector
Crosses four eras in the timeline

Volume 1 contains:
Knights of the Old Republic Volume 5
Dark Times Volume 3
Volume 2 contains:
Rebellion Volume 4
Legacy Volume 6

BSW4 = before *Episode IV: A New Hope*. ASW4 = after *Episode IV: A New Hope*.

FOR MORE ADVENTURE IN A GALAXY FAR, FAR, AWAY . . .

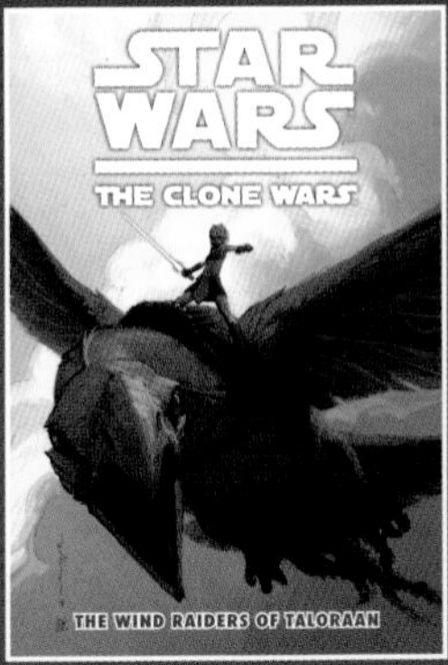
STAR WARS
THE CLONE WARS
THE WIND RAIDERS OF TALORAAN

STAR WARS: THE CLONE WARS—THE WIND RAIDERS OF TALORAAN
978-1-59582-231-4 | $7.99

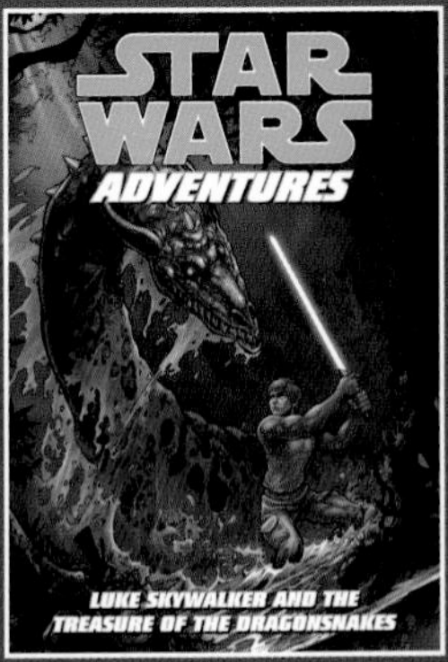
STAR WARS
ADVENTURES
LUKE SKYWALKER AND THE TREASURE OF THE DRAGONSNAKES

STAR WARS ADVENTURES: LUKE SKYWALKER AND THE TREASURE OF THE DRAGONSNAKES
978-1-59582-347-2 | $7.99

STAR WARS ADVENTURES: HAN SOLO AND THE HOLLOW MOON OF KHORYA
978-1-59582-198-0 | $7.99

STAR WARS ADVENTURES: PRINCESS LEIA AND THE ROYAL RANSOM
978-1-59582-147-8 | $7.99

STAR WARS ADVENTURES: THE WILL OF DARTH VADER
978-1-59582-435-6 | $7.99

STAR WARS ADVENTURES: BOBA FETT AND THE SHIP OF FEAR
978-1-59582-436-3 | $7.99

STAR WARS: THE CLONE WARS—SHIPYARDS OF DOOM
978-1-59582-207-9 | $7.99

STAR WARS: THE CLONE WARS—CRASH COURSE
978-1-59582-230-7 | $7.99

STAR WARS: THE CLONE WARS—SLAVES OF THE REPUBLIC
978-1-59582-349-6 | $9.99

STAR WARS: THE CLONE WARS—THE COLOSSUS OF DESTINY
978-1-59582-416-5 | $7.99

STAR WARS: THE CLONE WARS—IN SERVICE OF THE REPUBLIC
978-1-59582-487-5 | $7.99

STAR WARS: THE CLONE WARS—HERO OF THE CONFEDERACY
978-1-59582-552-0 | $7.99

STAR WARS: THE CLONE WARS—DEADLY HANDS OF SHON-JU
978-1-59582-545-2 | $7.99

STAR WARS: THE CLONE WARS—THE ENEMY WITHIN
978-1-59582-845-3 | $7.99

DARK HORSE BOOKS
darkhorse.com

AVAILABLE AT YOUR LOCAL COMICS SHOP OR BOOKSTORE

To find a comics shop in your area, call 1-888-266-4226
For more information or to order direct: • On the web: darkhorse.com • E-mail: mailorder@darkhorse.com
Phone: 1-800-862-0052 Mon.–Fri. 9 AM to 5 PM Pacific Time.

STAR WARS®

CLONE WARS ADVENTURES

Don't miss any of the action-packed adventures of your favorite STAR WARS® characters, available at comics shops and bookstores in a galaxy near you!

STAR WARS
CLONE WARS
ADVENTURES
Vol 4
STAR WARS
CLONE WARS
ADVENTURES
Vol 1
THREE NEW STORIES! ALL-JEDI ACTION!
STAR WARS
CLONE WARS
ADVENTURES
Vol 10
CLONES, DROIDS, AND BOUNTY HUNTERS IN FOUR FANTASTIC TALES!

$6.99 each!

Volume 1	**Volume 2**	**Volume 3**	**Volume 4**	**Volume 5**
ISBN 978-1-59307-243-8	ISBN 978-1-59307-271-1	ISBN 978-1-59307-307-7	ISBN 978-1-59307-402-9	ISBN 978-1-59307-483-8
Volume 6	**Volume 7**	**Volume 8**	**Volume 9**	**Volume 10**
ISBN 978-1-59307-567-5	ISBN 978-1-59307-678-8	ISBN 978-1-59307-680-1	ISBN 978-1-59307-832-4	ISBN 978-1-59307-878-2

AVAILABLE AT YOUR LOCAL COMICS SHOP OR BOOKSTORE
To find a comics shop in your area, call 1-888-266-4226
For more information or to order direct: • On the web: darkhorse.com • Phone: 1-800-862-0052 Mon.–Fri. 9 AM to 5 PM Pacific Time.
• E-mail: mailorder@darkhorse.com *Prices and availability subject to change without notice.

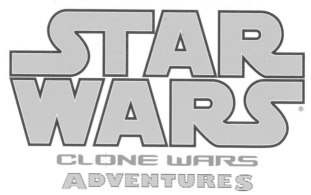

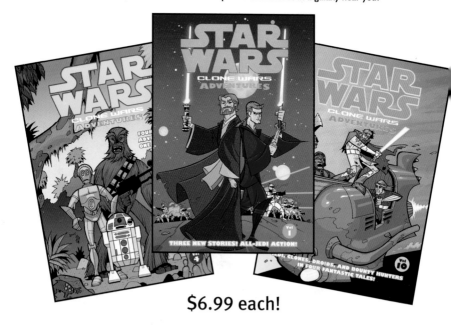